Great Awakenings & Other Plays

David Ewald

Also by David Ewald

The Thief of *That*

The Book of Stan

The Fallible: Stories

He Who Shall Remain Shameless

Copyright © 2026 by David Ewald

All rights reserved.

No part of this book may be reproduced in any form or by any electronic or mechanical means, including information storage and retrieval systems, without written permission from the author, except for the use of brief quotations in a book review.

ISBN-13: 979-8-9889795-6-2 (trade paperback)

Performing Rights: Applications for performance, including readings and excerpts, by amateurs and professionals should be addressed to the author at davidewald.net. No performance of any kind may be given unless a license has been obtained. Applications should be made before rehearsals begin. Publication of these plays does not necessarily indicate their availability for performance.

This book is a work of pure fiction. References to real people, events, establishments, organizations, or locales are intended only to provide a sense of authenticity, and are used fictitiously. All other characters, and all incidents and dialogue, are drawn from the author's imagination and are not to be construed as real.

for all the theater kids

Great Awakenings

Great Awakenings was given a professional staged reading on August 10, 2009, at the Crossroads Theater in Denver, Colorado as part of Paragon Theatre's The Trench. Director: Cathy Reinking. Producer: Wendy Franz.

The cast was as follows:

JILL..................**MICHAELA CULLEN**

AMANDA......**HANNAH MARIE HINES**

ELI...................**CURTISS JOHNS**

PAUL...............**STEVE BURGE**

Great Awakenings

ACT I — Friday Night

ACT II — The Morning After

TIME: May 1998

PLACE: The campus of a large religious university

SET: A two-person dorm room. Two twin beds are positioned on opposite sides of the room, and at center two desks with credenzas have been placed back-to-back so that they partition the two sides. On one desk is a Gateway computer, while the other, the desk closest to the doorway, is computerless. Behind the partition but still visible are a sink and a mirror, to the right of which is a door leading to an adjacent bathroom. On either side, at back, is an identically-sized closet with sliding mirror doors. Stage-left, just visible, is a large bay window that overlooks a mountain range. Stage-right is a door leading to the hallway. Throughout the room are assorted odds and ends associated with female college life.

CAST:

Jill, 18
Amanda, 18
Eli, 21
Paul, 19

Act I

Darkness.

Ocean sounds. The cries of whales. Waves crashing against the shore. The faint hiss of receding foam.

The door opens abruptly, throwing light from the hallway into the room. JILL and ELI stand swaying and laughing in the doorway, close. They are drunk.

As they stumble into the room the ocean sounds continue. A figure bundled under the farthest bed begins to move...

ELI: I still don't get why there's blood on the wall. Did somebody have their period?

JILL: You'll say anything. Aaaaanything!

ELI: You saw it. You pointed it out to me!

JILL: Sssshhhh...

ELI: Like you were proud of it.

JILL: Sssh! I told you, don't you remember?

ELI: Are we at the aquarium? Where's the otters? Where's the sharks? Where's that big ugly fin floating around?

JILL: Ssssh! I told you about....

ELI: Are we in a movie? I feel like we're in a movie. (*pause*) Action...camera...lights!

He flips the switch. The room goes garishly bright.

JILL: Stop it. No lights!

ELI: You want 'em on, don't lie to me.

JILL: You're such a big lughead. Just a big, big lughead.

ELI: You like me that way. You want me to carry you.

JILL: Huh?

ELI: Don't you? Like in the olden days.

JILL (*sobering up*): What are you talking about?

The figure under the covers is sitting up now.

FIGURE: Unnnnhh! Unnnnhhh!

ELI: Ah! It's alive!

JILL: Sssh! It's my roommate. I told you.

ELI: You told me everything. Everything but what I wanted.

FIGURE: That's rich.

The bedding falls away to reveal AMANDA in her pajamas. She squints and blinks her eyes.

JILL: Amanda! I thought you were...

Long pause.

AMANDA: Yeah.

JILL: I'm sorry.

AMANDA: No you're not.

JILL: I'm...not?

ELI: Sure she is. I am too! (*to Jill, whispering*) What are we sorry about?

In a huff Amanda gets out of bed, turns off the ocean sounds on her CD player, goes into the bathroom and slams the door behind her.

ELI: So that's—

JILL: You don't say anything!

ELI: But—

JILL: We're friends!

ELI (*sobering up*): Sure you are, sure.

Amanda comes out of the bathroom, gets back into bed, wraps herself up in covers.

AMANDA: Go away.

JILL: Amanda, is everything okay? I thought you were with...

AMANDA (*throwing off covers*): Everything *was* okay! Until now.

ELI: Wow. Oh man.

AMANDA (*to Eli*): Why are you still here? (*to Jill*) Why is he still here?

JILL (*to herself*): Why am *I* still here?

AMANDA (*pause*): What do you mean?

JILL: Nothing.

AMANDA: It's your room too.

JILL: I know.

AMANDA: I'm not telling you to spend the night on the street, Jill.

ELI: You can come over to my room...

Both women stare at Eli. Amanda is visibly shocked.

ELI: ...not for the whole night, I mean.

AMANDA (*to Eli*): Who are you?

JILL: He's a friend.

AMANDA: Some guy you met.

JILL: A friend!

AMANDA: Some guy you met *tonight*. (*pause*) Oh God, Jill. Are you drunk?

JILL: No.

AMANDA: You are!

JILL: Of course not!

AMANDA: Come here...

Amanda leaps out of bed and grabs at Jill, attempting to pull her close. Jill resists, beats off Amanda's hands and turns her head away from her prying roommate's encroaching face.

JILL: Stop it!

AMANDA: Let me smell!

ELI: Let her go!

AMANDA: Let me smell, Jill!

ELI: Hey! She doesn't—

JILL: Don't touch me!

AMANDA: Breathe on me! I have to smell your breath!

ELI: What are you, the first female breathalyzer?

AMANDA: As opposed to the male? Get out of here, imbecile.

JILL: Aaaah! Aaah!

AMANDA: There! I smelled it. I smell it...

JILL (*under her breath*): Fucking freak.

Amanda pauses on her way back to bed. She does not turn around but instead sits on her bed and stares.

AMANDA: God, Jill.

JILL: It's nothing.

AMANDA: So this is it.

JILL: I didn't even have that much. (*pause*) Amanda! What are you going to do, tell Sister Jost? Get me *excommunicated*?

ELI: I think I should go.

AMANDA: You should've gone a long time ago. What's your name anyway?

ELI: Eli. Not really nice to meet you.

AMANDA: Not really nice to meet you either. Maybe if it was under better circumstances, we could converse.

JILL: Jesus! Why do you have to sound like you're in a fucking novel!

Even Eli is taken aback by this outburst. He turns to leave.

ELI: Like I said.

JILL: Stay. Please.

Eli sees her look. He stays.

AMANDA: I knew this was coming. I knew.

JILL: Then why—

The phone rings. All three look at it. Jill looks at Amanda, who is closest.

AMANDA: Don't answer it.

After four rings the machine picks up and Amanda and Jill's voices come on. A standard greeting—but a cheerful one. Whoever is calling does not leave a message.

AMANDA: Remember when we recorded that?

JILL: I remember. (*pause*) Why didn't you answer it? Isn't it...

AMANDA: Of course. He's been calling all night. I won't talk to him.

Amanda rolls over in bed and hugs herself. Jill edges toward her roommate.

ELI: You know, somewhere in Africa right now, there's a kid crying over the body of his mother. (*pause*) I'm just saying.

JILL: Eli. I want you to stay. But please. Don't say anything stupid. Especially now that you're sober.

ELI: I'm going.

He opens door.

JILL: You're staying.

ELI (*almost out*): Now why would I do that?

JILL: Because when I'm done talking with Amanda I'm going back to your place with you. Like we talked about.

Eli enters the room fully and closes the door behind him.

ELI: Okay.

AMANDA: How could you do it, Jill?

JILL: How could *he* do it, whatever he did to you. Did he dump you?

AMANDA: No. Not yet. He got his calling.

JILL (*attempting to connect*): Oh that's great.

AMANDA: And we got into a fight.

JILL: But. You both knew.

AMANDA: I know. And...I was ready. Ready for two years without him. Of him living in Lithuania. And me writing him letters every day. Isn't that the way it is with us?

JILL: Oh Amanda...

AMANDA: But then I got this idea into my head. Why don't *I* go on *my* mission? I know it's not as long but I thought maybe, maybe if I make my intention known then by the time I get the calling he'll be six months in, and I may get placed in his city, or in a city nearby, or a country nearby, or I don't know. But I thought. I thought he'd still have eighteen months left and I'd have my full eighteen months to go and wherever we were, no matter where we were, we would finish together, and we could be on the same plane coming back together, and his family would be at the airport, all his brothers, and all my family would be there too, everyone together, and he and I would come out into the arrival hall, and when they took pictures of us we would take pictures of them, and then we'd get married, and have children and...and everything. Isn't that crazy?

JILL: Oh Amanda.

AMANDA: But then when I told him my idea, my dream, he got really mad. Said I shouldn't be a sister missionary, didn't I know, sister missionaries are losers and all the guy missionaries make fun of them. He didn't say—but I know he wanted to say—that he couldn't go out with me if I became a sister missionary.

ELI: That's messed up.

JILL: I'm sorry.

AMANDA: I'm a fool.

JILL: No you're not.

AMANDA: I'm a fool for thinking he was the one I was meant to be with. We weren't destined for each other after all. I prayed to Heavenly Father and—

ELI: You should get drunk with us.

JILL: Eli!

ELI: It's a joke! Just a joke, jeez...

JILL: He loves you. I know he does. He said so. (*pause*) Didn't he?

AMANDA: Why did you do what you did tonight.

JILL: Amanda...

AMANDA: No. I want to know. Because I've seen this coming. I just didn't know when or the reasons why you'd want to stray. Why you'd willingly choose a life of sin, away from your family. Away from Heavenly Father.

ELI: Oh here we go with the moralizing to sink a thousand ships. What we haven't already heard before.

JILL: Eli! Cut it out.

ELI (*to Amanda*): Don't tell me you've never fudged on the Word of Wisdom. Never took a sip from a beer...

AMANDA: Never.

ELI: ...hard cider...

AMANDA: No.

ELI: ...a little wine...

AMANDA: No way.

ELI: ...a wine cooler. Champagne. O'Douls...

AMANDA: No, no and...What's O'Douls?

ELI: What about coffee, tea, *Pepsi*...

AMANDA: Never, never, never.

ELI: Not even once.

JILL: Believe her.

ELI: You're telling me you haven't even once touched yourself.

AMANDA: What?

JILL: What?

ELI : You know.

AMANDA: That's it. Get out of here! Now!

ELI: I bet you've got a vibrator under your pillow. Jill, take that pillow away and you'll see. I swear!

AMANDA: Out! Who are you? (*pause*) Are you LDS?

ELI: Was. Am. (*pause*) Does it matter?

AMANDA (*to Jill*): How did you—how did you get drunk? You weren't in Salt Lake, were you? You can't get into any of those private places—you're not old enough!

ELI: But I am. The clubs aren't my thing, but I have a driver's license, and a truck. A big fat pickup truck that gets about twenty-five to the gallon. Drives like mad. It'll drive you from Salt Lake all the way to the western edge of Utah in just over an hour, no joke. Your eyes won't have time to tear up from looking at the salt flats on either side. Just the open road, the blue-on-black horizon, teeth of the land rising up, a little classic rock on the tape deck to calm the nerves, that what you're doing may be the last thing you do.

AMANDA (*to Jill*): And you say I talk like a novel.

ELI (*feeding off the attention*): Why the western edge? The first town across the Nevada state line is West Wendover. It's on Mountain Time, but it's as Nevada as they come. Just casinos, fast food joints and auto repair places. But if you look hard enough where the actual people of West Wendover live, you'll find it. On a little side street before the main exit takes you to the Rainbow, the Peppermill, the Red Garter, there's a little liquor store where the owner's real nice. Sell me anything I want. Not just another sad soul, you see. I got plans. I earn my money, and I like to spend it. "Work hard, play hard," that's my motto. Like to let loose a little bit, you know. I'm doing this for the love of my country! I'm not spending it on women. I'm not spending it on machines. I'm putting money into *his* register. I'm giving him a livelihood, a reason for being there! He and I talk for a bit and it turns out we come from the same place...So many sad souls escaping the desert for another. Our second great migration. I swear over half this guy's customers are LDS. All escaping. To West Wendover, Nevada! God's Country!

AMANDA: How dare you.

ELI: I'm willing to part with some of my stash for the likes of you.

AMANDA (*aghast*): You're a *student* here?

ELI: Oh yeah. Majoring in World Ambitions and Gluttony.

JILL: He's a returned missionary.

AMANDA: No.

ELI: Just got back. Well, a few months ago. The southern Spanish seaside town of Tarifa, free-based and raised.

AMANDA: Congratulations?

ELI: I was hoping my calling would be for a place by the ocean. I wanted to dunk as many heads under as I could.

AMANDA: No, really. Congratulations.

ELI: You don't believe me. (*to Jill*) She doesn't believe me.

JILL: She believes you.

ELI: It's amazing how many converts we had, and we were the only two at work in the entire town. There we were, cornering as many tourists as we could on the beach before the sun went down. And even when it did go down we stayed on the beach, the sand soft and cold between our toes. I have some back at my place—sand, I mean, not the toes. It's in a Ziploc bag, if you want to see it.

AMANDA: I'm not seeing any sand.

ELI: Why not? Let's go.

AMANDA: You're going to your apartment or whatever. I'm not. Now get. Out.

ELI: Get? Out? I was asked to stay here, so I'm staying.

AMANDA: As long as you're on my side of the room I can tell you to get out. Now.

Eli deftly steps across to Jill's side of the room.

ELI: Sanctuary!

AMANDA: Fine. I'm going then.

Amanda gathers up her blankets and pillows.

JILL: Amanda!

ELI: Good. And take your Symphony of the Sea while you're at it.

AMANDA: I will!

ELI: A regular Ishmael we got here. Half expecting a hook like a snow hill to be spouting off the starboard bow.

JILL: Eli, shut up! Amanda, where are you going?

AMANDA: Down. I'll sleep down in the study lounge.

JILL: That's ridiculous.

AMANDA: Until he leaves.

JILL: You're not doing that, okay?

ELI: All hands! All hands on deck! Will Master Starbuck be so kind as to hand the captain his looking glass so he may espy the great white—

JILL: Eli, for the last time stay out of it!

ELI: If you want me out of it then why do you want me here, huh?

JILL: Because I want to fuck you!

Silence. Amanda stands near the doorway, holding her blankets and pillows. She stares at Jill, as does Eli. The phone rings.

ELI: Do I have to get that?

He makes a move for the phone.

AMANDA: No—

But Jill beats them both to it.

JILL: Hello? (*pause*) Who is this?...No, it's not.

Jill looks at Amanda, confused. Amanda shakes her head adamantly.

JILL: No, she's not...Who? Oh my God. Paul?

AMANDA: Paul?

JILL (*covering phone*): It's Paul.

AMANDA: Not *the* Paul.

JILL: Yes, *the* Paul.

AMANDA: Paul from Anomar Paul.

JILL: Yes!

AMANDA: I didn't think—

ELI: —Who?—

JILL: —I know.

ELI: Who's Paul?

AMANDA: What does he want?

JILL (*into receiver*): Didn't you get my email? Oh. Well I thought. *Where*? Wait. But that didn't mean...No no, no. It's okay, I think. She'll be back, I just don't know when.

AMANDA (*more to herself*): Me? When will I be back?

JILL: It's just. Wait. I don't know. I have to call you back.

AMANDA: He wants to talk to me?

JILL: It's—okay. (*gets pen and paper*) I'm ready. Okay. Uh-huh. Okay. And that's. Oh. Okay. I'll call you back. I will.

Jill hangs up.

JILL: That was Paul.

AMANDA: I know. What's happening? He wants to speak to me?

JILL: Yeah. Kind of. He wants to speak with me too.

AMANDA: But he obviously asked for me first.

JILL: Let's not get into this again, okay?

AMANDA: I think we're going to have to if he's here. (*pause*) He is here, right?

JILL: He's here.

AMANDA: Here-here. In Provo.

JILL: In some cheap motel near campus.

AMANDA: What?

ELI: Hold on. So this guy who called—been calling—isn't your boyfriend? Not the guy who's going to Lithuania.

AMANDA: I guess not. (*pause*) I can't believe he actually called. And he's here.

JILL: Here-here. He...He wants to see you when you, uh, get back in.

AMANDA: And he asked for me first.

JILL: Amanda, don't you remember what we swore? What you made me do to him?

AMANDA: I didn't make you do that. That was your decision!

JILL: Your decision as much as mine.

ELI (*to Jill*): What did you swear? I gotta say this is really starting to creep me out here.

JILL (*to Amanda*): He wants to say something.

AMANDA: To me.

JILL (*pause*): Yes.

AMANDA: What? (*pause*) We shouldn't call him back.

JILL: I know, but don't you feel at least a little guilty for what we did to him, in the end? I thought of the summer.

AMANDA: Don't you think I thought of it too? We both did.

JILL: I know.

ELI: I sure as heck wish I knew. What's going on with you and this guy?

JILL: I have to call him back. He's at this motel and he doesn't have a long time, he said.

AMANDA: He's not... you know, *suicidal* or anything... like that... right?

JILL: I don't think so.

AMANDA: How did he get here?

JILL: He said he just drove here.

AMANDA: He drove here all the way from *California*?

JILL: He's determined. As always.

AMANDA: What are we going to do?

JILL: I have to call him back.

AMANDA: Let me call him back. He wanted to talk to me first anyway.

JILL: I would but.

AMANDA: I'm not in the room, am I?

Jill picks up the phone.

AMANDA: Don't, Jill.

ELI: Whoa. Is this guy a threat? Is there gonna be more blood on the wall out there? Is he like some knife-wielding maniac?

JILL (*laughs*): Hardly.

ELI (*loud, losing it*): Who is he then? What's this about what you swore and the summer?

He gets it.

ELI: Oh brother. He's your ex, isn't he?

JILL: Not really.

ELI: *Not really*?

JILL: He's just a friend.

AMANDA: A good friend. A—a childhood friend. Not one of us, not in our religion...

JILL: Norman Non—

AMANDA: —but a friend.

ELI (*to Jill*): And you shut him out.

Jill stares at Amanda, who looks away.

ELI: He probably thinks you turned on him. Both of you.

AMANDA: I didn't think it would hurt him. I should've seen how he was...

JILL: Sensitive.

AMANDA: Serious. What he and I went through with Brad...

JILL: I know.

AMANDA: We grew up together. All three of us. In Anomar.

ELI: That's...

AMANDA: It's almost near the ocean. Almost a fast-growing town. Almost incorporated in the county. It's almost everything you can think of, if you care to think about it.

JILL: He was there for me.

AMANDA: He was...

ELI: And now he's here. For you, obviously. Wanting exactly what I want, I bet. I can't blame him.

JILL: Eli, that's not it.

ELI: Then what is it then, huh. You want me here, you don't want me here, you want to have sex with me, what? Do you like me enough to care about me?

Silence.

ELI: Okay. Maybe I'm still a little drunk. Maybe it's the beer talking for me now, so I apologize if it is. But when I saw you over there on the sofa in the student center I just knew. I knew you weren't like every other girl I was expecting to find here. I didn't know why you were here.

JILL: I don't know why I'm here either.

ELI: So then I come over and say hi, real friendly like. And I mean it. Mean what I say. It's good for a guy to mean what he says every so often, right? Ask what you're reading. I like to read too. We get to talking, and I get to thinking this is a woman I could spend my nights with. Maybe not the entire night, because she could be...but she seems, yeah, she seems right. Just right. For me. And so we get into my truck, pop the clutch and head on over to my place. No way I'm staying in a dorm when I'm twenty-one and a returned missionary who wants to leave all that behind.

AMANDA: You said 'woman.' Why?

ELI: You didn't mind the place, right? I mean I admit it wasn't much to look at, still needed some shaping up. Well, some sweeping would have helped. But you at least didn't seem to mind. Sat back on the couch, said hello to my heathen roommate who, I swear, honest, is really never around, usually. Made yourself at home. Wonderful. Didn't say anything snide about the artwork—my artwork—I'd hung up, the attempt. And then when I offered you something to drink you got up and went right to the fridge yourself. Like you knew what I had, and you knew what you wanted. I liked seeing that. I liked seeing you walk. Is there anything more beautiful than a woman walking into a man's kitchen? If there is, tell me.

Jill has since placed the phone back in its cradle.

ELI: And I thought with you I could get out. Just cut away clean, you know. Not live this bullshit any longer. Like you wouldn't care that I had a case of beer in my fridge, and I hadn't spoken to my family since I left for Spain, and when I was in Spain I hated having to pound the pavement for Him, street to street, door to door, sometimes stall to stall. I hated converting the non-believers, pushing them into the waves and holding them under. I hated Heavenly Father. I wanted to go to Morocco, I could see it just across the Strait. To Tangier, if only for a day—and I did. And I wanted to tell you about that escape—that brief escape, because I felt you were good and noble and lovely, I knew all this and felt it too as I watched you bend down and pick a bottle out of the fridge.

JILL: I am good and noble and lovely. Thank you.

ELI: Don't thank me. Thank the place you're from. Thank the Church that brought you up right.

JILL: I'm sorry.

ELI: Now I am leaving. I won't spring this sucker trap set. That childhood shit goes deep, I know. This is really too familiar to me. If you need this guy here now...then what am I? Where do I stand? Right here, I know, but...

JILL: It wasn't supposed to be this serious.

ELI: Yeah, well, somehow I didn't see that smoke signal.

He leaves. Silence.

AMANDA: Are you still going to call him?

Jill hesitates before picking up the phone.

AMANDA: Jill, let me call him. (*pause*) He asked for me. He wanted to speak to me first.

JILL: I knew this was a bad idea.

AMANDA: It is a bad idea. Either let me call so I can deal with him or let's not call him at all.

Jill begins to dial.

AMANDA: Jill! Please. (*pause*) Just how badly do you want to see him?

JILL: I feel we owe him an explanation—for how we've behaved.

AMANDA: How have we behaved?

JILL: You can't admit it, can you? We've acted awful toward him, since the summer, that decision. Just awful. Like we're not his friends, but we are his friends. He just doesn't know—

AMANDA: It was for *our* friendship. To save it.

JILL: That's what you said.

AMANDA: You agreed—

JILL: It obviously didn't work, because now he's here and he's not going away. He won't ever go away unless we tell him why we've been so cold, so different than before. If we don't tell him he'll keep coming. You know how he can hold on. Do you really want to see him ten years from now, twenty years, still waiting for an answer? Do you really want to get another call in the middle of the night? I mean, do you? I'd rather not. He needs an answer, and I can give it to him. I should be the one to tell him the truth of what we've done.

AMANDA: He's not LDS.

JILL: That's what it's always been, hasn't it? (*pause*) He may not be one of us, but he's a friend, and you didn't share with him what I shared.

AMANDA: I shared *plenty* with him. Brad...

JILL: Brad. I know.

AMANDA: You weren't there that day. You didn't see him...like that...at the end.

JILL: You described it to me. I'm sorry you went through that. No one should have to.

AMANDA: I wasn't the only one. Paul...

JILL: And you think because you were both there—

AMANDA: It's *enough*, Jill.

JILL: 'You never know what is enough unless you know what is more than enough.' He doesn't know that.

AMANDA: He made me the star of his movies. He didn't even put you in the first one.

JILL: He filmed me.

AMANDA: When? Was it another movie? (*beat*) Jill? What *did* you share with him? Because I always thought...

JILL: I knew this was a mistake.

AMANDA: Then put down the phone. Don't make it.

JILL: I already did. (*off Amanda's expression*) This was the mistake, Amanda. Us living together. Me coming here. All this...mess. I knew it wasn't right, knew I should've gone to another college, or not gone to college at all—

AMANDA: —Don't say that—

JILL: —but I couldn't disappoint you. Jesus, I can't disappoint anyone. Maybe that's why I'm calling him now.

AMANDA (*in a more demanding tone*): So what did you share with him.

Silence.

AMANDA: You had it with him, didn't you? That thing...

JILL: It's called sex.

AMANDA: That thing we can't do before marriage if we ever hope to reach the Celestial Kingdom. Jill, it's—

JILL: It's a sin, I know. I'll take my chances.

AMANDA: You know the consequences, yet you *did it* with him.

JILL: Not with him.

AMANDA (*pause*): But you did do it.

JILL: Yes.

AMANDA: With who? (*pause*) With *whom*, Jill?

JILL: Someone you don't know. He's gone now, so it doesn't matter.

AMANDA: (*visibly hurt*): Tell me his name.

JILL: I said it doesn't matter. He's gone. I don't even know where he went or his last name even.

AMANDA: That's how you like it. Not knowing them.

JILL: I've only done it once. Jesus, you make it sound—

AMANDA: Were you drunk? I bet you were drunk. I bet you were throwing up all over him as he...while...while it happened. I bet you were so blind you never saw his face. Puking on his body, your body—

JILL: Oh shut up.

AMANDA: On your parents...

JILL: Shut up!

AMANDA: All over your grandmother in the corner and

your brothers and sisters and nieces and nephews and your Testimony that you gave you knew to be true!

JILL: My Testimony that last day was bullshit, Amanda.

AMANDA (*in tears*): He changed you. If we'd never known him...

JILL: But we do. And you can't let him go just as much as I can't.

AMANDA: Not true. (*beat*) It's because of your fathers, that's what it is. I wasn't there when he came over to comfort you. I wasn't there when you did the same for him. And what did you say? What else did you do?

JILL (*beat*) Oh God. You think...Amanda, I barely knew him, when he was there for me.

AMANDA: What about last June, when his dad died? What did you do together then?

JILL: How could you even think that?

AMANDA: Of course I can think that! You just told me you had it with some stranger. Why wouldn't you practice with Paul? Touch him, let him feel you up. Get your head-start.

JILL: My father had just *died*. He came over and we talked. We hugged, for a long time. It seemed so long...I didn't want him to let go. There was nothing else...no hands, no touching, no kissing, nothing that you think. And when his father...when his father fell...I had to do the same. We were older, but it wasn't any different. The hug. We didn't want to let go. We didn't want to stop talking then or finish what we had.

AMANDA: What I could never be a part of.

JILL: Be glad your father's still alive.

AMANDA: You don't think. Jill. You don't think...You don't think Paul killed—

JILL: No. I do not. Now drop it.

Jill dials the number.

JILL (*into receiver*): Hello? Paul. Yeah, sorry. Sorry it took so long...Yeah, that's true. I know. Um, yeah, she is...

Jill looks at Amanda as if to offer the phone. Amanda shakes her head and continues to hug and console herself.

JILL: ...but she can't come to the phone. Yeah, she's...well, not available. But she will be tomorrow. Yeah, that's better for us. It's late and...okay, good. Um, what would you say to...maybe ten o'clock? Is that okay? Yeah, exactly. Okay so it's...Oh, you do? But not...okay. So we're in DT—Deseret Towers, Building One. Top floor, room 601. It's at the corner, the very end of the hall...Exactly. Can't miss it. (*long pause*) What's that? Oh...yeah, don't worry. She will...All right. See you tomorrow. Bye.

Jill hangs up. Amanda has since composed herself.

AMANDA: He really wants to see me.

JILL: He may really *want* you, too, for all I know.

A beat and Amanda gets it. She is upset.

AMANDA: I never thought you'd turn into this, Jill.

JILL: Well I have, and I'm dropping out.

AMANDA: Dropping out of what?

JILL: Of college. Here.

AMANDA: What? You're WHAT? You can't...

JILL: I've got all the papers ready. I haven't formally declared but I will soon. Monday—why not?

AMANDA: But.

JILL: It's more than the Church. Of course it's that, but it's also my future. I want a career. I want to explore my talents, and I can't do that here. The program I'm in is an approximation of what I dream of doing, and it's never going to get me there. So I'm looking at other schools. I think first I'm going to take some time off, maybe a year. It was the wrong idea to throw myself into college along with every, everyone else. Maybe I'll go live in another country, I don't know. I certainly won't have Mom's support. But I will have my brother's. There was a time when I thought I'd have yours too.

AMANDA: Our plans...

JILL: That you created, and I went along with. I didn't want to deny you. You were too happy.

AMANDA (*sullen*): Thanks.

JILL: You're going to have a great life, Amanda. You might not see it now but you are. You're going to be fine with Joseph, and you're going to marry him, and you'll have however many children it takes—

AMANDA: —I resent that—

JILL: —to fulfill your obligations. But that's not me. Never was. I thought maybe when I was twelve, thirteen, but no, not even then. Not even at baptism. Paul made me see that. I didn't have to have sex to see that, but I did. Try to understand. (*pause*) I think you think we're sisters.

AMANDA: We are sisters!

JILL: In title maybe, but not in spirit. Not anymore.

AMANDA: How did this happen? How could I have possibly hurt you to the point where you're saying these awful, ungodly things to me? We made a promise even before Paul. We made so many promises...apparently worth nothing.

JILL: No. Far from it. They were worth everything. We both know that and—

AMANDA: —Then—

JILL: —still you ask.

AMANDA: Then why?

JILL: Because you listened but you refused to reason, refused to see that people, even your best friend, could change. That there were other opinions that might go against your beliefs. That there might be another way in, or no way in at all—and if that's the case then guess what? *That's okay*. It's okay, it really is. It's okay. I'm telling you this now. There might be no way in at all, and it is okay.

Jill collects her toothbrush from the sink. She heads for the door.

AMANDA: Where are you going?

JILL: I'm going to spend the night with him.

AMANDA: *Paul*?

JILL (*laughs*): No, of course not. I told you Paul and I never...I'm going to spend the night with Eli.

AMANDA: Oh.

JILL: Yeah. *Him*.

AMANDA: So you're going to "sleep with him."

JILL: That's what a woman usually does when she meets a guy she likes.

AMANDA: There's that word again. That funny word.

JILL: What?

AMANDA: Woman. (*pause*) We're not women. We're too young to be called that. Or to call ourselves that.

JILL: What do you think we should call ourselves?

AMANDA (*pause*) I think it sounds funny. That's all.

Jill opens the door.

JILL: I'll be back by ten tomorrow.

AMANDA (*a threat*): I'll tell Paul.

JILL: I can't stop you, so go ahead. I'm ready for him. He *should* be ready for me. He knows me well enough.

AMANDA: He'll be so angry.

JILL (*smiling*): He asked for you first, remember?

AMANDA: Whore.

JILL (*almost out the door*): I'm ready for that, too. (*pause*) Please don't touch my things tonight while I'm gone.

AMANDA: What would Sister Jost say to you if she found out your brother is a homosexual and you hadn't told her? What will your father say when you see him finally? Think about it. How will you explain Jacob's absence? When he calls for his son, and his son doesn't come, how will you explain that to your father? How will you? Will your mother even be there? How will they feel toward you then? Will they wonder what other secrets the two of you were keeping from them? And in this world, the here and now, your mother, alone. Think of her. Will she feel at all comfortable with you, let alone him? Will she maybe not return your calls, your hugs, let you know you're not welcome in her house, disown you just as Heavenly Father will disown you both?

JILL: That's not the way it works.

AMANDA: It *is* the way it works! And you know it. You always have. That seal's already been broken; you can't fix it or get rid of it by hiding the truth. Someone has to tell her.

JILL: You wouldn't.

AMANDA: I wouldn't. But I know others who would. A call can always be made.

Silence. Jill tries to contain herself at the door. Finally she closes it and walks toward Amanda, who rises to confront her.

JILL: You are the most innocuous, despicable—

AMANDA: I *am* going to save you, Jill.

JILL: You can't save me.

AMANDA: I survived a *shooting*. I can surely save you.

JILL: By blackmailing me.

AMANDA: It's not blackmail. It's the truth.

Jill SLAPS Amanda across the face.

JILL: Save that, bitch. You're so good at remembering things.

AMANDA (*clutching face*): Oh my God. Oh my God!

JILL: Yeah. It won't be the last time.

AMANDA: I hate you! I was only trying to help!

JILL: I never wanted it! I never wanted the calls, the lessons, the gifts, the readings, the sleepovers, the secrets, the photos! I never wanted *any* of it! (*pause*) I never wanted our friendship.

AMANDA: You don't mean that. That's not true.

JILL: No. You're right. It's not. (*pause*) Why am I listening to you, anyway? You can't hurt me.

AMANDA: I can.

JILL: You're not even a real human being.

Amanda stares at Jill uncomprehendingly.

JILL: I mean, *you know*....

AMANDA: Oh, screw you. Don't.

JILL: *Quid pro quo*. We're finally talking.

AMANDA: Sh-shit on you.

JILL: That's it. That's more like what I expect to hear from someone who's not really a Saint. At least not the way she should be. Someone whose parents couldn't have children —God knows why they weren't blessed with the ability—so she had to be born in a science lab, unnaturally. She and her two sisters, all they could manage.

AMANDA: God...damn you. F-fuck you.

JILL: Not even a real—

Amanda PUNCHES Jill in the face. Jill holds her nose; blood trickles from between her fingers.

JILL: Ah, God...

Amanda pushes Jill hard in the chest.

AMANDA: You're not coming back after you leave tonight!

JILL: Oh I am. I just need to get everything I own and then I'm moving.

AMANDA: Good!

JILL: You just be out of the room when I'm in.

AMANDA: I will!

JILL: I'll be gone, I'll be gone by tomorrow night. That's a promise.

AMANDA: Why don't you just leave now? Oh, but then you wouldn't get to *fuck your fellow whore.*

Jill backs toward the door.

JILL: I need some space...some breathing room. And then we'll see.

AMANDA: Get the fuck out!

JILL: You see sex as a scary thing, as work...

AMANDA: You don't know what I see.

JILL: ...but it's not. It's the most beautiful thing. So terribly beautiful.

Amanda throws a book at Jill, who allows it to peg her before she exits the room, closing the door behind her. Amanda falls onto her bed and sobs for several moments. Gradually she gets control of herself, enough to open her diary. She writes furiously. As she does, the lights dim and soon go dark. In the darkness, Amanda rises and crosses to center stage. Spot on Amanda as she speaks.

AMANDA: But you do remember. I know you do. The night you walked from town all the way to my house without fear, without fear of retribution or the headlights from cars or the helicopters overhead. And you woke me with a tap on the glass, the secret sound. I remember, I hope you do too. The way we pretended to have horses, riding until dawn when our backyards weren't big enough. The way you scolded me for turning the wheel too soon and staying in the car when you thought it was going to crash. You and him watching me like our parents, and all I wanted that night was the safety of bodies and the inability to see. The smell of the parking lot underfoot. The way you put your fingers to your lips as I leaned out the window, your hands on my stomach as I slid out and onto the path circling the house. Slid out the way I should have at the very beginning. And then we were off and racing, and who would ever think to follow the two invincible sisters, invisible through the trees as we jumped and ducked and dived to blaze a new path to the creek bed, our hideout, our lair, so high now in early summer, swollen and mischievous, like a smile with the moon's teeth easing up from it. I remember. We could just see it ahead, along the right bank and hanging from the strongest branch. Just a swing, they would say, just an old wooden swing hanging from a tree—but not to us. To us it was our stallion, that debonair steed. Only room for one of us on it, and you chose me that night—why? Why would you do that. I could not have pretended any more than the next rider, the next girl. The next sister. And yet it was my moment to escape, to flee, to strike out and thunder on until sunrise in hopes of warning the others before it was too late. And so I slid into the saddle, and I rode. Your hands on either side of me holding the reins, making sure I didn't fall. Your shoves and pulls, shoves and pulls coming so fast I felt brave enough to sing, to laugh, to cry out, to let you cut my hair. And I could not have known that the stars were watching, I could not have known that the whispers in the hall and the voice in the trunk were my own, beyond the creek bed and the forest and the countryside, beyond town and church and men and men. I could not have known beyond that night that the day would be so harsh; that, exposed, we would be forced to kneel even when we had nothing to say. And are you dancing on stage with me now? I'm afraid even that is a memory. I'm afraid I could not have avoided this, or any of this. That pride was the problem inherent in our past, one remembers the other forgets, the place and time, people and pleasures. It makes no sense to write any of it down; it'll only be burned, won't it? I am afraid. And I want those moments again.

Lights down on Amanda. In darkness she crosses back to her bed and continues writing in her previous position. Lights up.

Amanda stops writing. Spent, she closes her diary and puts it away. She stands up from the bed and retrieves a small piece of scratch paper. Her eyes on this paper, she dials the number.

AMANDA (*into receiver*): Hello? Hi, Paul. It's me. It's Amanda.

Blackout.

End of Act I

Act II

The same. Sound of someone taking a shower from behind the closed bathroom door.

A knock on the door leading into the dorm room. Some moments pass before the knock sounds again.

Nothing. The shower continues. The door to the dorm room opens and in walks PAUL reading a post-it note. He is dressed sharply: a dark sport coat over a button-up dress shirt; dark slacks and dress shoes complete the outfit. He sets the post-it note down on Amanda's desk then goes over to the bathroom door and listens. The shower runs with little to no variation in the sound of the falling water. Paul makes like he's going to say something into the bathroom door then thinks better of it. He moves toward Amanda's desk and sits in her chair, looks all around. Eventually he wakes up the Gateway desktop computer and clicks on a folder, surveying its contents. The shower shuts off. Paul quickly puts the computer in sleep mode and crosses to Amanda's bed. There he sits on the edge, his legs crossed, his hands clasped and resting on one knee. He averts his gaze as Amanda steps out of the bathroom wearing a towel tight around her body and another towel wrapped around her head. She smiles at Paul, who still has not looked at her.

PAUL: Should I close my eyes?

AMANDA: No need.

Casually Amanda goes over to the joint dresser she shares with Jill and, with one hand (the other still holding the towel), she selects the necessary undergarments. Then she goes to her closet, opens it and picks out a black dress that Paul seems to recognize. He watches. With clothes in hand Amanda disappears back into the bathroom. She shuts the door behind her, though not entirely. Paul remains seated. The bathroom door opens all the way and out steps Amanda wearing the tight, form-fitting black dress.

PAUL: I didn't think I'd see that on you again.

AMANDA: It's only been a year.

PAUL: I'm surprised you kept it. I didn't think...

Amanda observes him, a wry smile spreading.

AMANDA: No. You didn't think.

Silence.

AMANDA: So.

PAUL: So.

AMANDA: Are you still making movies?

PAUL: Not now. Not since I changed.

AMANDA: Changed how, Paul?

PAUL: You'll find out soon. But really I'm good. Is it all right to say I'm good? Is that allowed? Because I wasn't so good the last time we talked. (*beat*) When was that?

AMANDA: Oh, months, I think.

PAUL: September. I'm pretty sure it was September. You'd come back from only a month here to trumpet your triumph.

AMANDA: What triumph?

PAUL: Your boyfriend, remember?

AMANDA: You seem to remember perfectly.

PAUL: We were at your house, and you'd just shown me his photo, the head shot. (*beat*) Is he still your boyfriend?

Amanda approaches Paul. She dries her hair as she speaks.

AMANDA (*chiding*): Now Paul

PAUL: I suppose what I should've said was "How's that working out for you?" (*beat*) Sorry.

AMANDA: It's working out fine. Why are you curious?

PAUL: I'm always curious about those things. I—I care about you, Manda. I still do. That's why I drove out here, really. You should know that.

AMANDA: Do you care about Jill? Are you curious about her too?

PAUL: She sounded awfully distracted on the phone last night.

AMANDA: That's because she was with someone. He was standing in the room when you called. Standing over there by the door, actually. Then they left together, for his place.

PAUL: Oh.

AMANDA: To...you know, spend the night together.

Paul nods, taking this information in.

AMANDA: Do you still care about her? Are you still *in love* with her the way we figured you were last year, last summer...

PAUL: And you both were so scared...

AMANDA: *We* were scared?

PAUL: Scared of what would or might happen, that's all. Even she was scared. I felt the fear in her body, but I didn't back down or turn away. Didn't seek out someone else, though I could have, I know that now. I know now I'm ready. I'm ready for someone else.

AMANDA: Is that why you came here, to tell us you were ready for a girlfriend? Jeez, Paul, why didn't you save yourself the trip and just tell us over the phone?

PAUL: No, it's not that. I had a girlfriend. She was great but...it didn't work out. We broke up.

AMANDA: I'm sorry. Did—

PAUL: She ended it.

AMANDA: Oh.

PAUL: Just recently. Like, a couple weeks ago.

AMANDA: I'm sorry, Paul. I'm sure it hurts. In fact, I know it does.

PAUL: It used to hurt. I'd say up until a few days ago it did, acutely.

AMANDA: How long were you together?

PAUL: Since November. Thanksgiving. You could call it the Turkey Pick-up, I guess. She was having a party at her place. Her parents and sisters were out of town so—

AMANDA: Paul. You know I don't want to hear *that*.

PAUL: She'd just turned seventeen so—

AMANDA: Paul, I do not want to hear this!

Silence.

AMANDA: I don't want to hear about your night with her, or any of your nights with her.

PAUL: Because you're—

AMANDA: Don't say it. If you say it I'm going to throw you out of here. (*beat*) I'm not.

PAUL: That's right. You have a boyfriend. It didn't sound like you did last night when you called, so late. (*pause*) Why the dress now?

AMANDA: Why the suit? Are we going to prom all over again? Oh but that's right. You really wanted to take Jill, your true love. So you asked me. What a great night that was.

PAUL: Certainly memorable.

AMANDA: You remember I let you dance with her. I never asked: How was it?

PAUL: It was like dancing with a piece of furniture you want moved from one end of the room to another.

AMANDA (*beat*) Why are you here? (*beat*) Because if it's to belittle me or hurt me with the past or go out and *score* with some *chick* who I'm sure you can find on campus somewhere here—there are always some who stray—then I don't want any of it and I want you out of here. Seriously, Paul. Tell me what's up or *go*.

PAUL: How long before Jill gets here?

AMANDA: Do you need...

PAUL: I'd like her to be here too, if possible.

AMANDA: 'If' is the operative word, really. Who knows when she'll be back. We had a fight last night.

PAUL: Oh.

AMANDA: We really got into it.

PAUL: How much into it?

AMANDA: Like...

PAUL: Like tearing hair and clothes? Gnashing teeth?

AMANDA: She slapped me and I hit her.

PAUL: Amanda!

AMANDA: Maybe it was the other way around.

PAUL: Jeez. How—

AMANDA: It was a fight, okay. I don't want to go into it. Things were said.

PAUL: Yeah but—

AMANDA: Hurtful things. Secrets. (*beat*) Very hurtful things...were said. (*pause*) There was some gnashing teeth, if that helps.

PAUL: So...she's not coming back?

AMANDA: She'll come back. Her stuff's still here.

PAUL: But you don't know when.

AMANDA: Paul. Does she have to be here? Whatever you have to say, why not say it to me? Is it such a big deal?

Paul's look says it is.

AMANDA: I was kind of hoping...?

PAUL: What.

AMANDA: I was kind of hoping it would just be you and me.

PAUL: It is just you and me.

AMANDA: You know that's not what I meant.

PAUL: But it's what you said.

AMANDA: Now you're being mean.

PAUL: I can be mean.

AMANDA: I didn't know.

PAUL: I can be spiteful.

AMANDA: In all the time we dated...

PAUL: I can be vindictive. I can be jealous. I can be petty. I can be sinister. I can be lustful.

AMANDA: You can also be obsessive. I know that much.

PAUL: So we'll wait. Waiting for Todog.

AMANDA: What?

PAUL: Nothing.

AMANDA: I thought it was over. I really did. But obviously you're upset and there's nothing I can do about it, even though it's me you're upset with. Are you upset with her?

PAUL: I'm not upset.

AMANDA: You just said you are.

PAUL: I didn't say that.

AMANDA: You agreed you're being mean.

PAUL: I said I *can* be mean.

Pause.

AMANDA (*lowering her voice*): Paul, is it—is this...Are you gay? Is that what this is?

Paul waits a beat before bursting into laughter. Palms slapping knees, body doubled-over, the works.

PAUL: *No...*

AMANDA: I just thought...

Paul continues laughing.

AMANDA (*exasperated*): I just thought since you were so serious, you couldn't tell me over the phone, had to be in person, and you dressed up nice...

At the utterance of "you dressed up nice" Paul bursts even wider. He doesn't seem able to stop.

AMANDA: Paul! Stop! Stop it! You're scaring me!

Paul's laughter subsides.

AMANDA (*calmly*): I just thought from what I know about you, and hearing that your relationship ended. Your girlfriend ended it...

Paul is once more serious.

PAUL: So just because a relationship ends does that mean the guy is gay? Or if he ends it does that mean his girlfriend, the dumped, is a lesbian?

AMANDA: No. No. Of course not, but... (*beat*) Paul, you can tell me if you're gay. I—Jill's brother's gay. Jacob.

PAUL: I know.

AMANDA: You do?

PAUL: She told me. Months ago. I said I was okay with it, and that's the truth.

AMANDA (*beat*): I'm okay with it, too.

PAUL: "Love the sinner, hate the sin," right?

AMANDA: That's right.

PAUL: Choose the Right. (*pause*) I'm not gay, Manda. This isn't a coming out—not in that sense.

AMANDA: Then what sense is it? In about a minute I'm going to lose all patience I have le—

Sound of a key in the lock. A knock on the door. Amanda looks panicked. She checks her watch, mouths, "Jill" to Paul and then hurries over to hide in her closet. She closes the sliding mirror door behind her. Through all of this Paul appears dumbfounded.

The door opens; Jill enters.

JILL: Oh.

PAUL: God your face.

JILL: She didn't tell you.

PAUL: That she punched you? Uh, yes. She did.

JILL: Is she...in there? (*indicates bathroom*)

PAUL: No.

JILL: She's gone then.

PAUL: Yyyes.

JILL: Good. I can leave in peace.

Jill goes over to her closet, opens the door, pulls out clothes. Item after item lands on her bed.

PAUL: Where are you going?

JILL: I'm sorry you have to see this.

PAUL: Yes but I—

JILL: How long ago did she leave?

PAUL: Well...

JILL: I know you won't understand, but the sooner I get out of here before she gets back...

PAUL: You didn't answer my question though.

JILL: Do you want to see the other side of my face look like this? I don't know what she's liable to do if she sees me again.

PAUL: She says you slapped her.

JILL: Tell me which is worse.

PAUL: I think they're both terrible.

JILL: But not equal.

Silence. Jill resumes her task.

PAUL: How about if I, uh, help out? Help speed things up a little...

Jill looks at Paul, nods. He comes over to her side of the room. Close now, they pull and fold.

PAUL: I never thought I'd be in your dorm room helping you pack up and go.

JILL: Thank you, by the way.

PAUL: It's really happening. I thought you'd stay friends forever.

JILL: Yeah, well. I got sick of being a child.

PAUL: I understand.

JILL: Do you? Do you really?

Silence.

PAUL: Does it hurt?

JILL: Like a bastard. But the swelling's gone down, believe it or not. I soaked in a tub most of last night.

PAUL: Whose tub?

JILL: I gotta go, Paul. Thanks again for the help.

PAUL: So...

JILL: You haven't changed your email address, right?

PAUL: I came here to see you, you know.

JILL: No. You came to see her.

Silence.

JILL: Why else would you ask for her when you heard my voice on the other end? I was there. You could've told me then. (*pause*) Tell me now.

PAUL: What.

JILL: *You* know. Your big announcement.

PAUL: How do you know I have something to say.

JILL: Paul. You always have something to say. You just don't say it. (*pause*) So. Say it.

Silence.

JILL: Well you didn't dress up and drive all the way out here to sleep with me...

PAUL: Fair enough.

JILL: Like you wanted to.

PAUL (*pause*): I['m]—

Eli pushes the door open and pokes his head in.

ELI: You done? (*to Paul*) Oh hey. You must be...

Paul reluctantly shakes Eli's outstretched hand.

PAUL: The guy who called last night.

ELI: Paul.

PAUL: Right.

ELI: Well I'm Eli, and I'm here to help Jill make a clean break.

PAUL: All right.

ELI: You okay with that?

PAUL: Sure.

ELI: Positive?

JILL: Eli...

ELI: It's just I don't want to get clocked too. The male version and all.

JILL: Eli, stop it.

PAUL: I'm really not like that. I'm not very...um, physical. Physically aggressive, I mean.

ELI (*smiling*): Well I am. Physical and physically aggressive. So don't be messing around with me!

Eli assumes a faux-fighter's stance and takes harmless joke-jabs at Paul, who goes along with it half-heartedly.

ELI: Right?

PAUL: Okay. I won't.

ELI: So let's get out of here. You got everything?

JILL: Everything that matters, I think...

ELI: Looks like it'll take a couple trips. That is unless Paul here wants to help out.

PAUL (*pause*): Sure.

ELI: Truck's parked around the building. Only place I could find a spot.

JILL: Oh Jesus. My scarf.

ELI: But it's May, honey. What do you need a scarf for?

JILL: It's *my scarf*. It was my grandmother's and she gave it to me, and her grandmother gave it to her.

ELI: So...

PAUL (*more to himself*): Do scarves last that long?

JILL: It was a *gift*, it traveled overland from Illinois to Utah in—

ELI: 1847.

JILL: Yes.

ELI: And that still matters to you?

JILL: *Yes*.

ELI: Then let's find it.

JILL: She has it. I let her borrow it and I never got it back.

ELI: Well it's gotta be here. Unless she mailed it to Siberia.

JILL: It's in her closet, I bet.

PAUL: Um...

Jill goes to Amanda's closet and opens it.

JILL: Oh God!

AMANDA: Ah!

ELI: Oh God!

JILL: Jesus!

AMANDA: Sorry! (*pause*) He didn't tell you?

PAUL: *I* was supposed to tell her you were in there?

JILL: You knew she was in there?

PAUL: Yes!

AMANDA: Yes!

ELI: What were you doing in the closet?

JILL: What are you doing in the closet wearing your prom dress of all things?

AMANDA: I...thought I'd put it on for Paul. (*quickly*) I didn't think you'd come into my closet looking for my scarf...

JILL: It's not your scarf!

AMANDA: You gave it to me!

JILL: That didn't mean you could keep it. How many things of yours have I borrowed and eventually given back?

AMANDA: Eventually...

JILL: How long?

AMANDA: It wasn't a thing to be borrowed. It was a gift!

JILL: Give it. Now. (*pause*) Give it and I'll go.

Amanda reaches into her closet.

AMANDA: Indian Giver.

ELI: Damn. You know the historical background of that slur, I hope.

Amanda comes out with the scarf.

AMANDA: A slur, huh. If you have to ask, you know the answer.

ELI: I wasn't asking. I was hoping.

AMANDA: And I was remembering when I last heard it. (*to Jill*) Here. Take it.

ELI: Are you crying?

AMANDA: *No.*

ELI: Your eyes are sure watery. You all can see that, right?

JILL: Eli. Leave her be.

AMANDA: There's no way you're going to the Celestial Kingdom.

ELI: Tell me something I don't know.

AMANDA: I knew somebody. He last used those words, Indian Giver. They were some of the last words he ever said.

ELI: Now that's something I didn't know. (*pause*) Who was he? Boyfriend?

AMANDA: Does everything have to be boyfriend and girlfriend with you?

ELI: Pretty much.

JILL: It was a friend. He was a friend.

AMANDA: Two years ago this summer.

ELI: Damn. I'm sorry.

PAUL: I was there too, when it happened. It was a real tragedy.

ELI: Where'd you say you're all from again?

JILL: Anomar, California.

ELI: Sounds exotic.

AMANDA: It's really not. We could do so much better.

PAUL: All of us.

ELI: But, yeah. That term...I won't bag on it again, seeing what it does to you.

AMANDA: Thank you, Mister High and Mighty.

ELI: There's no need for that now. I'm not the one using an outdated term from the time of the Ute.

AMANDA: Who?

ELI: The Ute. The people who, you know, were first here in this state. Before it was a state. Before the White Man came in his many wives.

JILL: Eli!

AMANDA (*to Jill*): He's utterly irredeemable—and you know it.

ELI: You're right. She does know it. And she wants it. (*to Jill*) That's what I love about you.

AMANDA: You don't love her.

ELI: I didn't say I did. It's *something about her* I love.

PAUL: Oh.

ELI: That surprises you. (*pause*) Why?

Silence.

PAUL: I should tell you why I'm here.

AMANDA: Finally!

PAUL: Now that you're both in the room. (*pause*) There's no chance getting you to leave, is there?

Eli shakes his head.

PAUL: Didn't think so. Okay. (*pause*) Okay. I'm here to tell you about the change that's happened in my life recently. It's a big change and I'm hoping you'll approve. I'm pretty positive one of you will at least. It would be great if you both would because you both had so much to do with it. Influenced it, really.

AMANDA: You've given up filmmaking, you told me that much.

PAUL: It's far more special than filmmaking ever could be. I had to give that up if I wanted this new life.

JILL: Oh God.

AMANDA: What?

JILL: Paul, you can't.

AMANDA (*to Paul*): What can't you do?

PAUL: I'm converting, Manda. Everyone: I'm converting.

JILL: Paul, please.

PAUL: What?

JILL: I'm saying don't.

PAUL: You actually care.

JILL: Of course I care. It's not right.

PAUL: Then tell me why it isn't.

Long pause.

JILL: There are things you should've asked about. Remember when I gave you that chance, last year, on our way back from the ward? I asked you if you wanted to know anything, and you—

PAUL: And I said what?

JILL: You said nothing, pretty much. No wonder you can't remember. I got nothing from you that day. That was the time to ask about serious things, deeper things...

PAUL: It wasn't my time for that.

JILL: And now is? What happened? It's not you.

AMANDA: His girlfriend.

JILL (*to Paul*): Ex-girlfriend?

Paul's silence answers for him.

JILL: Did you hear me that day? You must have heard

what I said last: If you go back a second time they'll try to convert you. You were interested...

PAUL: I was, and I did. Hear, I mean. I heard. (*pause*) I went back.

JILL: You mean right after...and before we...

PAUL: Not that one. I went to another ward, near campus.

JILL: I see.

PAUL: What do you think of this, Manda? Haven't heard from you yet.

AMANDA (*pause*): It's uh, it's interesting.

ELI: 'Interesting'?

AMANDA (*sharply*): Yes.

ELI: You've known this guy for, what, a *lifetime*, from what I remember hearing. Dated him. Dropped him to move on, but you didn't move on, did you? You clocked my girlfriend in the face, and the next morning you invite him in to deliver the biggest news of his life so far and all you can say is 'interesting'? Interesting—

PAUL: —Hey man—

ELI: —is for coffee table books.

PAUL: Man.

ELI: Interesting is for those nature documentaries you watch while flipping channels at five in the morn—

PAUL: Hey! Man!

ELI: The name's Eli. Remember?

PAUL: Eli. You like to hear yourself talk?

ELI: Not you too. All right, put up your little dukes big boy...

PAUL: I'm not fighting you. Just answer the question: Do you like to hear yourself talk?

ELI (*pause*): You could say that, yeah.

PAUL: Good. I do too.

ELI: Who doesn't, right? Talking is one of the last best things we have. (*pause*) You gotta admit the word 'interesting' is—

PAUL: It's not her fault. (*to Amanda*) It's not your fault. I just thought you'd be happy for me. I figured if anyone *you*...

AMANDA: Then is this because of...?

PAUL: Jill I figured. I suspected...

JILL: I didn't murder anyone, Paul.

PAUL: I didn't murder anyone either. (*beat*) I hope you know what I mean.

Jill nods.

AMANDA: But. If that's why you're doing it...If that's the real reason why you're converting...

PAUL: Why do you think I'm converting.

Silence. All eyes on Amanda.

AMANDA: Because of what we went through together. Seeing Brad...on the ground like that.

PAUL: In the grass.

AMANDA: Your backyard.

PAUL: And you prayed. You didn't go get help, you didn't call 911...You prayed.

AMANDA: That was help.

PAUL: I know. I know that now.

AMANDA: Then that's why—

PAUL: Not entirely.

AMANDA: No?

PAUL: No.

AMANDA: Because of your...Because of your father. Because you feel guilty, and you want to save him. I don't think you killed him, I'm not saying you killed him, but I do think what you're doing it's not right, because *it's not genuine*. (*pause*) Is that the reason?

PAUL: That's not the reason. (*to Jill*) I thought once you were in you were always in. I thought that especially after Pioneer Day last year, when you denied me.

AMANDA: Denied?

PAUL: When she refused to have sex with me.

ELI: Oh shit.

JILL: I didn't...really...deny you. You knew.

PAUL: I didn't really know. That's the thing. But I know now. I know that you didn't care about me, you don't care about me now—

JILL: That's not true!

PAUL: And that you can't care about *any* guy. *Any guy*.

Paul stares at Eli, who doesn't look away.

PAUL: What did you do last night?

ELI: None of your fucked-up business what we did.

PAUL: You didn't get what you wanted. You're not going to get what you want.

Eli launches himself at Paul, his fists pummeling the taller, younger man. Amanda and Jill struggle to pull the two guys apart.

JILL: Stop it! Stop!

AMANDA: Stop! Cut it out!

After more shouting and pushing and pulling, Jill and Amanda manage to force Eli off of Paul, who appears relatively unscathed.

ELI (*to Paul*): You have no *idea* what I want!

PAUL: You've got a massive temper, man.

ELI: This isn't a *temper*. This is about sticking up for what you know is right and *who* you know is right. She's my girlfriend, you chode, how can I not defend her? She needs me—and it's totally okay if she doesn't, but she does, I feel she does. Would you if she were your girlfriend? Oh, but that's right, you don't *have* a girlfriend, so you're gonna go join a religion just so you can *get* one!

JILL (*near tears*): Stop it! Stop it! Stop it!

ELI: Babe!

PAUL: I...didn't say anything, Jill.

JILL (*to Eli*): I'm not your *babe*. I'm not your girlfriend.

ELI (*long pause*): Huh.

JILL: I'm sorry, but I'm not.

ELI: I thought...well, huh. I thought since, you know....

JILL: I'm sorry I led you to believe—

ELI: You didn't lead me to believe. You led me to hope. And that's worse than believing.

AMANDA (*to Paul*): I think you should leave.

PAUL: I will. (*pause*) I will.

He does not move. No one does.

ELI: I figured since you're, you know, *moving in and all*...

JILL: That's just a temporary thing until I—

ELI: So I'm temporary.

JILL: Not temporary, no. You're great—

ELI: I don't want to be great. I want to be *your boyfriend*!

Silence.

ELI: There was no future. Since I met you there was never going to be a future. There was just going to be your messed up asinine past.

JILL: Maybe, eventually, it would work out...

ELI: How could you not say we're together, have a future together, after you said all those things to me, after we said all those wonderful things to each other...After we *did* those things last night...

JILL: We do have a future together.

ELI: This is the future, right now. And you've denied it. (*pause*) I can't do it, you know. I tried...I really, honestly did the best I could...

JILL: I know.

ELI: To *respect* you. I specifically did not use the word 'love' because I didn't want to freak you out. I had no idea it was the 'g' word that got to you.

JILL: I did the best I could too.

ELI: Uh-huh. I see why you didn't leave anything at my place...You probably didn't leave anything in the truck either.

Jill's silence confirms this.

ELI: What should I do? Where should I go? (*beat*) I'm not asking you—any of you.

Eli turns and leaves the room quickly. He shuts the door softly behind him.

Silence.

AMANDA: Okay, Paul. That's your cue.

PAUL: I've accomplished nothing, really.

AMANDA: I meant you need to go. Now.

PAUL: I'm going to be amongst you, Manda. I'm about to be baptized. I went through the conversion talks with the missionaries. I went to church. I read the scriptures, and I prayed to Heavenly Father. I'm going to be as you are. I'm going to have a chance. Now aren't you relieved? Aren't you glad for me?

AMANDA: I...I am.

Jill, seated on her bed now, scoffs as Paul looks at her hard.

PAUL: I couldn't have stopped that car from hitting your father's.

JILL: I didn't expect you to. (*beat*) I wish I could have stopped your father from falling. On that hiking trip.

PAUL: End of summer—

kicking up dust

on the way to your house.

AMANDA: Paul, I'm not—

PAUL: It wasn't the end of summer, actually. That came later, of course. That last walk down the long road. No, what I'm talking about came a little earlier, another walk, at the height of summer, with the heat pushing through the windows of every building and vehicle in our little town. (*pause*) It wasn't as bad, that walk, not nearly as bad as what they went through to get here. You know, *them*...

JILL: Tell her. Go ahead.

AMANDA: Tell me what?

JILL: You want to know what we did? I don't care what we did.

AMANDA: Paul?

PAUL: It was Pioneer Day, and I was again walking to her house, camcorder in hand. I was trying to get the scene right, just right...And she was there waiting on the porch, ready to tell me off but instead she let me in. The fact I needed her, I wanted her for my movie flattered her. And why wouldn't it? What other options were there in Anomar, in her Church, her family? She cut my hair, even though I didn't need a haircut. I liked the feel of her fingers on my scalp, the light scrape of her nails against my skin. It was...arousing. I was aroused. I'm not ashamed to say that. I'm not official yet, and so I won't be ashamed.

JILL: How convenient—

PAUL: Listen! We went into her room, where I'd once held her baby nephew on my chest and waited for the phone to ring. She didn't want to go in there, but I insisted saying it was where the scene needed to be shot, in the female protagonist's bedroom.

JILL: Ready for Hollywood.

PAUL: I was pushy, and I was prodding, the camera stood in for me, it *was* me, and I'm sorry but. I filmed her, like I'd come over to do.

JILL: On my bed.

PAUL: You looked perfect, the phone in your hand, talking.

JILL: I wasn't saying anything, Paul.

PAUL: I wrote the words.

JILL: I don't remember any of them. (*pause*) You moved on me.

PAUL: I was finished.

JILL: You were nowhere near finished. Hollywood...

PAUL: You did kiss me.

JILL: I felt I had to.

PAUL: On the bed we kissed. Lost in kisses, as if they would be enough. (*beat*) Isn't it true that you never know what is enough unless you know what is more than enough? I know who said that now. I said it.

Wait. Don't take it off. But I did. Everything. Everything except my skivvies—and she was still fully clothed, hidden from me. And what were we to expect? What then? So silent, when what I wanted most from her were words.

JILL: God you are so hateful.

PAUL: You said I could, and so I did. You allowed me.

And there I was: naked by your side, on your just-big-enough bed, naked like my father was on his first time with. (*beat*) Now. Now for you. And when I pressed, she relented by giving me a choice: the shirt or the jeans. Shirt or jeans—which is it gonna be? Fifty-fifty chance, a winner in every try...

AMANDA: She was probably...

PAUL: It surprised her what I chose. She even said it did after I'd taken to standing on the other side of the room, in front of the exit, incredulous at her refusal to follow through. How should I have felt? How would you feel? I'd made the wrong choice apparently: it was the shirt—and possibly the bra?—that was okay to come off, not the jeans. Not them. How was I supposed to know? How was I supposed to know that my fifty-fifty chance was not two sides to an all-winning coin but rather a win-or-lose situation, and I lost.

JILL: You had to lose. How could you...

PAUL: But here's what I really want to know: if I *had* chosen the shirt (and possibly the bra?), if you had taken that off would the jeans have followed? Or was it never going to happen? (*pause*) I know you can't answer. I know you don't want to answer. I asked too much of you. I'm sorry. You should've known I would pick the pants. You know me well enough to know what my choice would be. But how insulted I felt—offended, bare before you, shrunken, withered but ready, while you lay *protected* next to me in passive judgment. Safe behind your *clothes*.

JILL (*near tears*): I wasn't passive. I was raging.

PAUL: Good.

JILL: And the rage threatened me just like it threatened you.

PAUL: Good. That's what I was hoping to hear. That's

what I was thinking about as I went through the talks. That you felt for me. That you felt *something* for me.

JILL: I did. I did.

PAUL: And I: embarrassed, insulted, offended. All washed away as of soon. (*to Amanda*) We were never lovers but I can still tell you a dream: In it you and I are bouncing on a trampoline, only the trampoline is a circus net and below us is the whole world, with everyone looking up at you in your dress, and you flashing everyone and laughing about it wildly and joyously....and a song from some sad musical is playing above, and I thought of you on stage, singing, your cheeks flushed and puffing, I thought of you both tap-dancing with the black armbands and no one in attendance. It's not enough to recount a dream; you have to believe it as well.

AMANDA: I was going to say—Paul—I was going to say: I'm not your friend. I'm sorry, but I'm serious. I don't think I can be your friend.

PAUL: I'm going to be one of you.

AMANDA: That doesn't mean—that wasn't your reason. You're not converting because you want to be my friend. You don't want to be closer to me. You don't care about me. Even with what we went through together, you don't.

PAUL (*beat*): That's right. (*pause*) I'll tell you my reason. One night when I was fifteen my family and I went to see a musical in the city. It was a Sunday and we had dinner afterwards, in one of those fancy restaurants on the water. Our car was parked at the opposite end of the wharf, so we had to walk this great distance to get there and go home and that walk seemed to take forever, it was dark and the path was not well lit. My father and I were in this pretty amazingly good mood, so we stuck close together. We even laughed now and again. But afterwards...afterwards my mother let us have it. How could we have walked *ahead* of her and my sister, so far ahead of them that night. Didn't we understand our duty as *men*? Hadn't we seen what was around us?

Men—unsavory, unpleasant men—had caught up to my mother and sister and were closing in, encroaching on their space, while my father and I chortled on ahead unaware. And how would we have felt had we gotten to the car and turned around only to find our wife and mother and sister and daughter missing, absconded? Would we have felt less like men and more like monsters? Would we have felt free?

After I heard the truth of that night I took stock. I stayed in my room. I thought of everyone I knew and went over what I'd said to them and how they acted toward me. I decided that I didn't care about any of them—not even my mother and my sister did I truly care about. I realized I had always been walking ahead, walking ahead of everyone, trying to catch up to my father, who walked ahead of even me. Could I stop? Did I want to stop, turn around and at least look back? Did I have that ability in me to change?

I decided I did not. I was not capable of stopping; I would always walk ahead. And if I was always going to walk ahead why shouldn't I walk with those who are right and good and true. The one true. The best. Why not? The caring would come later, if at all.

Silence.

JILL: I have to say, Paul...I—I can't be your friend anymore either. It's just...too much, everything. I hope you find happiness.

PAUL: I know you will.

AMANDA: I can't be there for you. I know I promised once but...

PAUL: You will be there for me, eventually. (*pause*) I should go.

AMANDA: Yes, you should.

PAUL: Well, goodbye.

AMANDA: Goodbye.

Paul lurches forward, arms outstretched, searching. Amanda backs away.

AMANDA: Don't.

PAUL: It would mean so much to me.

AMANDA: You need help.

PAUL: I've found it. (*pause*) Jill?

Jill, not looking at him, shakes her head slowly. Paul addresses both women.

PAUL: Despite what you think, I have found it.

He turns and leaves the room, neglecting to shut the door behind him.

Amanda goes to the door and shuts it. She turns to Jill, who has not moved.

AMANDA: Jill?

JILL: My choice.

Amanda waits.

JILL: It was my choice.

AMANDA: I know.

JILL: And if he didn't like it he could've just gone and tried to fuck someone else.

AMANDA: 'Tried.'

JILL: Are they all like this? I mean, God, are they even *out there*?

Amanda approaches her.

AMANDA: But he didn't try...there was only us. (*pause*) It's strange to think he was that obsessed. Scary really. Because, you know, he's not that bad-looking, and he was smart and in all those clubs and classes...He kinda could've had anyone—just about anyone. Instead he chose us. (*pause*) What does that say about us? (*long pause*) Is it the religion or the people?

Jill suddenly breaks down and begins to cry. Amanda observes her coolly.

AMANDA: You were strong.

JILL: I had the right.

AMANDA: You had *every* right. You still do.

JILL: But you're wrong. I'm sorry: you are. He couldn't have had anyone. It wasn't in him. His confidence—his lack of confidence...

AMANDA: What does that say about us?

JILL (*gaining composure*): You understand.

AMANDA: I'm sorry about your face.

JILL: I'm sorry about the slap. I'll never—

Amanda shakes her head. Then: a knock at the door. Jill jumps a little. The women look at each other. The knocking continues. Amanda slowly goes to the door and peeks through the spy hole. Although surprised, she does not open the door. She quietly makes her way back to where Jill is seated. Together the women wait it out.

MALE VOICE BEHIND DOOR (*off-stage*): Amanda? Are you in there?

Another sharp series of knocks. At last, they end. Sound of footsteps receding.

Silence.

JILL (*low voice*): How are we going to get rid of him?

AMANDA: It was, um. It was Joseph.

JILL: Oh, Amanda. You shouldn't....

AMANDA (*pause*): Good. You stopped. Maybe he will too.

JILL: I thought...

AMANDA (*pause*): Remember when it was just us, and we were driving around the back roads, the uninhabited unexplored roads, and nothing mattered much, we didn't have to buy books, we didn't have to read, we could just *talk*.

Jill waits.

AMANDA: And we were talking about where we would go—not where we could go but where we *would* go. And we were listening to that song...

JILL: That song...

AMANDA: What was that song called?

JILL: "Going to California."

AMANDA: With the wailing in the background.

JILL: Was it wailing?

AMANDA: It wasn't?

JILL: I don't think it was. It was more like a, a moaning. I think.

AMANDA: You must not have heard the wailing. (*pause*) Do you remember where we wanted to go?

JILL: The places...

AMANDA: All the places, like—

JILL: Spain.

AMANDA: And Morocco. We could travel light in Morocco.

JILL: Heavy in Spain. Because of all the food.

AMANDA: And the clothes. Don't forget all the clothes we'd need in Iceland...

JILL: Land of the Midnight Sun. Or was that—

AMANDA: Denmark? Greenland? Does it matter?

JILL: It did matter.

AMANDA: It *does* matter.

The phone rings. Jill goes to answer it.

AMANDA: Don't. Not this time.

Jill stops. The phone rings a few more times before the answering machine picks up. The greeting comes on followed by the beep and then...

JOSEPH (*off-stage*): Manda, hi, it's me. I tried your room but I guess you weren't around. I thought you'd be back now because I checked all our places and I couldn't find you. Did you leave for the weekend or something? Your parents said you didn't say anything to them about that...Anyway, I really want to talk to you. It's important. I'm sorry. I want to see you again.

Sound of a beep.

JILL: What are you doing?

AMANDA: I'm doing something new.

JILL: This is important, Amanda. He's important to you. Isn't he?

Amanda waits.

AMANDA: It *will* matter. But that's not the 'it' I mean.

JILL: Okay...

AMANDA: Let's go.

JILL: Where?

AMANDA: To Spain.

JILL: You want to go to Spain, as in now?

Amanda nods.

JILL: Oh, God.

AMANDA: You don't want to?

JILL: No, it's just...I'm going to have some trouble seeing myself as a sister missionary.

AMANDA: We're not going as sister missionaries.

JILL: How much money do you have?

AMANDA: Enough to get there. How about you?

JILL (*nodding*): Enough.

The phone rings. Amanda gets up and goes over to it. She unplugs the answering machine. The phone continues to ring as Amanda comes back to Jill and sits beside her, close. After several more rings the phone stops.

AMANDA: Let's go.

JILL: You'll have to tell them, you know.

Amanda waits.

JILL: Aren't you scared?

AMANDA: Are you?

JILL: I don't know what's out there.

AMANDA: I don't either. But. At least it'll be up to us to find it out.

The phone rings. Neither young woman moves to answer it. They remain close, staring out the window toward the mountains. The phone rings. And rings.

Silence.

Curtain.

Her Kiss

TIME: Saturday, August 30 - Sunday, August 31, 1997

PLACE: A mini-mart and gas station on the outskirts of Anomar, a small town in north inland San Diego County.

SET: The action of the play takes place entirely inside the mini-mart/convenience store area of the gas station. In the center of the stage is the counter. At the front of the counter is the cash register, and overhead is a rack containing various brands of cigarettes. To the right of the counter, somewhat in the background, is a stand on top of which are containers for coffee, a coffee maker, filters, cups, etc. Just to the left of that, still somewhat in the background, is a standing rack containing pastries and sweets. Rows of goodies are seen stretching in the far background.

Although they are never seen, the front doors of the mini-mart slide open and can be heard off-stage when a buzzer (or electronic bell) sounds. Characters enter and exit stage-right.

The interior of the store is always well-lit.

CAST:

Brent, 23
Paul, 19
Mrs. Jenkins, 50
Tom, 17
Ian, 18
Trish, 27

Her Kiss

SCENE 1

Close to eleven at night. BRENT sits hunched behind the counter, writing in a spiral-bound notebook. Next to him is a radio, a backpack, and a large fountain drink. The place is quiet; no customers.

Brent glances at his watch then goes back to writing. Sounds of a buzzer and doors sliding open. PAUL enters. Like Brent he is dressed in a light blue standard-issue short-sleeved work shirt, but unlike Brent he wears a thin striped tie under and around his buttoned collar (Brent has his shirt partially open to reveal a white undershirt). Paul takes a moment to look around before going over to Brent at the counter.

PAUL: Hey.

BRENT: What's happenin'. Can you believe it? Some shit, huh.

PAUL: What happened?

BRENT: Didn't you hear? About Diana?

PAUL (*beat*): Who's Diana?

Brent stares.

BRENT: Diana. The Princess of Wales.

PAUL (*beat*): Oh. Princess Diana! Really? Did something happen?

Brent goes to put the notebook and pen in his backpack.

BRENT: Guess you didn't catch the news.

PAUL: I'm not much into news, really. I was listening to, uh, my mix-tapes on my way over here.

BRENT: Lost in your own little world...that's all right.

As Brent speaks he starts to close out his register.

BRENT: You're not the first kid I've seen like that. Not caring what's going on in the world.

PAUL: Hey, I care. Of course I care. What happened?

BRENT: She's dead, man. Princess Diana died in this ugly car accident in Paris—

PAUL: Wow. Just happened?

BRENT: Pretty much. She was running from reporters—again. They chased her into this tunnel—I guess she was in this car with Dodi—she wasn't driving, the driver was driving —and they crashed in the tunnel.

PAUL (*lost*): Dodi...

BRENT: Dodi Fayed. Her *boyfriend*.

PAUL: Huh. They all died?

BRENT: She died. Dodi died. The driver died. Pretty sure the bodyguard's gonna die. The car was pretty unbelievably mangled, you know.

PAUL: Wow. I mean, I guess that's...

BRENT: Everyone died except the reporters. Fuckin' paparazzi.

PAUL: That's the word for them?

BRENT: Yeah. You never heard that? You are young. (*pause*) Can't believe I'm handling money while talking about this. You know.

PAUL: Yeah.

Silence.

BRENT: Maybe it'd be different if you actually *saw* her get married. How old were you in July '81?

PAUL: Um, I was almost three.

BRENT: Well I was seven. And I remember sitting there in front of the TV, between the coffee table and the couch, my mom next to me, we were spooning peanut butter right out of the jar and watching this unbelievably beautiful wedding. The church ceiling—you couldn't even see the ceiling it was so high up. It was kind of like how a wedding would be in ancient medieval times, you know. With the attendants and the knights and the high priest...Almost expected Merlin to make an appearance, but maybe that was because I'd seen that *Excalibur* movie not too long before. Anyway, all the British royalty were there. Everyone. The cameras were on Diana twenty-four-seven, even then. It was fantastic. I'm sure they're going to put a tape out now of the wedding, if they haven't already, now that she's dead, the creeps. (*pause*) But as I was watching this perfect wedding play out I started thinking more about my mom. She loves Diana too, more than me. It was kind of like my mom was seeing herself in Diana then, during that wedding, imagining herself in Diana's dress, under that veil. She needed to be there, I think. We were alone with the peanut butter, you know. And my mom had kinda missed that part of her life, it was something she could never have but she could get close to it through the screen, you know? And she kept dipping her spoon into the peanut butter jar, and I did that too, and we'd almost finished it all off by the time the ceremony was over. The entire time my mom didn't say much, but I knew she knew it was something special, she wanted to be Diana, to be in this perfect life for once. (*pause*) But you didn't see that, did you?

PAUL: Pretty hard when you're two.

BRENT: Anyway. To go from that scene...to the one on the radio now...It really shakes you. Makes you think. (*pause*) Everything's gonna change after this.

PAUL: What do you mean?

BRENT: I don't know. Everything. If they don't put the paparazzi in jail then we'll become the paparazzi.

PAUL: Us? I don't...

BRENT: Crazy, huh? I've been writing about it pretty much since I heard.

PAUL: You write?

BRENT: Yeah. Do I look like I wouldn't?

PAUL: No, it's just—

BRENT: If there's one thing I can't take it's being judged.

From out of his backpack he takes the notebook.

BRENT: Been judged my whole life it feels like. I may not be going to *college*, but then does *everyone* need to go to college? (*reading from journal*) "Diana. Did you kiss Dodi? Before the fatal impact did you have one last chance for one last, sweet, sincere kiss? To say your final goodbyes through the most basic act we know?"(*pause*) "Diana. Your name is beautiful enough. I saw you at your wedding, I will see you at your funeral. Is this the future? Will I always see you? I won't forget your face—they'll make sure I won't. Got that? You're not going away. You can't just leave us. You're as much a part of us as we are of you. Got that? Diana. You think death is an ending—well I say it's the opposite. You wanted to fly out of that car, fly out of our lives? It's not gonna happen. I need to see you. I love you. You're ours."

Silence.

BRENT: I bet you're gonna write something to someone famous someday. Someone who's died.

PAUL: Mother Teresa.

Brent laughs.

BRENT: Mother Teresa. That's a riot. She's gonna live forever. What about your mom?

PAUL: What about her.

BRENT: I'm just saying. In your life your mom's probably famous. A star. Didn't you write one of those reports in elementary school where you had to talk about the most important woman in your life?

PAUL: I think I wrote about my teacher.

BRENT: Well anyway...The register's all ready for ya.

PAUL: What about a girl you like.

BRENT: A girl I like?

PAUL: Or anyone. I mean...do you have a girlfriend?

BRENT (*beat*): Nah. You?

PAUL: Yeah. Kind of.

BRENT: Kind of isn't yeah. Is she or isn't she?

PAUL: She isn't. But we shared a...a moment, last month. (*pause*) We got close. (*pause*) Really close. And she's coming here tonight and...

BRENT: And you want it to happen. Here in the store.

PAUL: I'm not saying that!

BRENT: What are you saying then? You're waiting for this kind of girlfriend who isn't your girlfriend to enter the store so you can...what?

PAUL: I don't know.

BRENT: Better figure it out before she gets here. Don't be surprised if she doesn't show up.

PAUL: Why wouldn't she?

BRENT: Cause she's in *mourning*. Along with the rest of the world. Cause she knows some things are bigger than her or you.

Brent slings his backpack over his shoulder, takes his drink and radio and heads out.

BRENT: Good luck tonight, man. Whoever you're with.

Brent exits, leaving Paul alone at the register. Lights down, spot on Paul. As he goes around the counter he takes off his tie, which is revealed to be a clip-on, and slowly unbuttons his dress shirt (he too is wearing an undershirt). He holds the tie and stands in front to address the audience directly (NOTE: Paul will do this at the end of each subsequent scene).

PAUL: He was right about my mom. She is, in a way, famous. Not physically. She was no beauty queen or runner-up for the Miss Anomar pageant. But she has a beauty of her own I can see, though it wasn't so clear then. (*pause*) When I was really young she read me this book called *The Runaway Bunny*, about this kid bunny who keeps telling his mother different ways he'll run away from home, and every way he says he's going to leave the mother has an answer for, so she'll always be there for him, to find and catch and bring him back, safe. But I don't know if it's safe. Maybe it's smothering. (*pause*) When I told her I'd be working the graveyard shift, eleven at night to seven in the morning, Friday and Saturday, last weekend in August, two weeks before I left for college, she flipped, like I knew she would. Said something to the effect of "What do you need to prove to people you don't even know?

All you're going to prove to them is that you can be ventilated." A coworker of mine had been roughed up in the store the previous Sunday, so I could give her that, but I couldn't give in to her demands to quit a job she'd been so adamant about me getting in the first place. Even with college a breath away... (*pause*) I felt I could do it. I kinda had to do it, actually. I wanted to do it. I didn't want to come home. (*pause*) Even with my dad...gone only two months at this point, I couldn't bring myself to go home, go to my mom. My sister was back at college, start of her junior year. I knew my mom needed me, but I needed Jill. I needed her again. She'd been there for me in June, when he fell...and again in July, sort of, when I...The first kiss we shared had been the first kiss for both of us. It was special. I wanted more. Was it wrong to want more, the summer she turned eighteen? (*pause*) I thought of Amanda a little. We'd shared so much, Brad and...homecoming and prom and...my films. But I couldn't touch Amanda the way I could Jill. Amanda was younger, true, but she was also destined. Jill was...unpredictable. That unpredictability freed her. I'd like to say she convinced me, but the truth is only I'd convinced me. And I wasn't going to say no.

SCENE 2

Almost one in the morning. The inside of the mini-mart remains vacant except for Paul, who sits on a stool behind the counter and reads (his tie is back on and his shirt buttoned up again—this will be the case at the start of each subsequent scene). Contemporary music plays softly overhead. After a few moments, the phone rings. Paul looks at it, not sure if he should answer.

PAUL (*into receiver*): Hello? Oh, hi, Mom. How are y—Oh. It's uh...slow, actually. Yeah, pretty slow. Well, they have this new system outside where people swipe their credit cards. Yeah, it's not too bad...You doing okay? I mean yeah—I know. I'll make sure to write down any license plates, don't worry about that. Yeah—me? No. I'm—what's that? Oh yeah, I don't think I'll have to. I'll be fine. Just gotta—okay, yeah. I will. Me too. See you later. At seven, yeah. Seven-thirty, probably. Bye.

Paul goes back to reading. Sound of the buzzer and sliding doors. MRS. AMELIA JENKINS enters. She is short, very thin, her hair in a bowl-shaped cut. Her skin is tan and weathered. She wears a leather jacket, leopard print skirt and high heels. Stumbling, she makes a beeline to the back of the store, where she proceeds to yank on the doors to the glass case containing the beer. Finding the case locked, Mrs. Jenkins shrieks and stomps.

PAUL: Ma'am. Ma'am! The alcohol's locked down at midnight.

Mrs. Jenkins turns and stumbles up to the counter.

PAUL: Mrs. Jenkins?

Mrs. Jenkins leans on the counter. Paul draws back.

MRS. JENKINS: Pack of Virginia Slims. Those aren't locked down, I hope.

PAUL: Isn't it...It's like, one in the morning.

MRS. JENKINS: And I'm *old*. Is that what you're saying, former student of mine?

PAUL: No. I'm saying...um, you're my English teacher.

MRS. JENKINS: *Former* English teacher.

PAUL: Still...

MRS. JENKINS: I know, I know. An English teacher. But the year I've had, Paul...

PAUL: I know.

Paul looks at the register awkwardly.

MRS. JENKINS: Surely you could open up that case in the back for just long enough for me to fish out a—

PAUL: I can't, Mrs. Jenkins. I know what your year has been like, believe me, I do, but...

MRS. JENKINS: You're a good egg, Paul. But you're still just an egg. (*beat*) I just have to get through tonight. Now give this customer what she asked for.

PAUL: But the liquor—

MRS. JENKINS: Christ, Paul! Not the liquor. The *cigarettes*. You'd think you didn't get a five on the A.P. exam.

Paul reaches for a pack.

PAUL: You know about that.

MRS. JENKINS: I'm always the first to know the scores, Paul. I wasn't surprised.

PAUL: Thanks. Uh, dollar ninety-eight, please.

MRS. JENKINS: And thank you.

PAUL: You sure you don't want to...

MRS. JENKINS: What, Paul. *Not* go home?

PAUL: Not drive. Which I guess means not going home.

MRS. JENKINS: That's not a good idea.

PAUL: You could stay here until...

MRS. JENKINS: Until I'm sober.

PAUL: Yeah. Or...less drunk?

MRS. JENKINS: I'm not drunk, Paul.

PAUL: Oh...

MRS. JENKINS: Maybe a little. A little less sober.

PAUL: I see.

MRS. JENKINS: I see I'm not convincing you. That's what I see. Are you going to call the police on me?

PAUL: I don't think I should, but.

MRS. JENKINS: You don't want to lose your job.

PAUL: You could kill someone, Mrs. Jenkins.

MRS. JENKINS: I've already killed someone, Paul.

Silence.

MRS. JENKINS (*tears forming*): I didn't mean that. (*beat*) I did mean that.

PAUL: Mrs. J....

MRS. JENKINS: It was this weekend a year ago. Close enough to it. That's why I was out. I didn't want to be home. I was out remembering with friends. I wasn't alone.

PAUL: I'm glad you weren't alone. I'm sorry. I should've stopped him. Al—

MRS. JENKINS: *Don't* say his name! Don't you dare speak that murderer's name.

PAUL (*pause*): I'm sorry. I know. I forgot.

MRS. JENKINS: You forgot. You *forgot.*

PAUL: That's not what I meant. I...If I'd just—

MRS. JENKINS: There are always the 'if's, Paul. If *I'd* kept him at home that day, after he...I wanted him home, after he did what he did...to that man. I thought about keeping him home. I should've. If I'd taken him and Tyler and gone into town, or down the hill, or anywhere away from the Gems, that would have...But no. If we lived in town instead of within walking distance of you, he might never have met you, and then he'd be alive.

Silence.

MRS. JENKINS: But he'd still be dead.

Silence.

MRS. JENKINS: There's a special providence in the fall of a sparrow.

PAUL: If it be not now, 'tis not to come.

MRS. JENKINS: If it be not to come, it will be now.

PAUL: If it be not now, yet it will come.

MRS. JENKINS: The readiness is all.

PAUL: Let be? (*beat*) I miss him. I hope you know that.

MRS. JENKINS: I know you do, Paul.

PAUL: What do you...What do you think of religion, Mrs. Jenkins?

MRS. JENKINS (*beat*): An effective means of mass control. Leading to the end of the world, someday.

PAUL: You really think that? (*beat*) Of course you think that. (*pause*) Do you think religion helps at all? Like when someone dies?

MRS. JENKINS: Like my son?

PAUL: Yes. You know he and I, last summer—

MRS. JENKINS: His last summer. But go on.

PAUL: He and I started reading the Bible. Starting at the beginning. (*beat*) We didn't get very far.

MRS. JENKINS: I know he was reading the dictionary, front to back. I wasn't aware he had any interest in the Bible.

PAUL: He had interest. I was getting him interested. Along with the dictionary he figured why not the Bible?

MRS. JENKINS: Why are you telling me this, Paul? Are you finding God? Getting religion? Are you going to save me because you couldn't save him?

PAUL: No I just...

MRS. JENKINS: You weren't *allowed* to stay alive that day one year ago. No higher power had a hand in keeping you safe. You simply lived that day. And my son died. (*beat*) I was looking forward to teaching him. Challenging him. In A.P.

PAUL: The Badger hasn't come back, has he?

MRS. JENKINS: We don't talk about him either. Now there's a man ripe for religion.

PAUL: Why were you...

MRS. JENKINS: Why was I ever with him?

PAUL: Yeah. Why? Because you must've known.

Mrs. Jenkins stares at Paul.

MRS. JENKINS: The things we do when we're young.

PAUL: If you don't want—

MRS. JENKINS: I was angry, when I was young. Angry at my parents. *They* were religious. I would have none of that. (*beat*) But at college, without them in my life, I had to fill their absence with *something*.

PAUL: Someone.

MRS. JENKINS: Not the Badger. Not yet. But men. At college, there was the beach and there were the men.

PAUL: I'm going to your college, you know.

MRS. JENKINS: I thought you were going to that low-tier school in Orange County.

PAUL: I decided against that. I thought about the beach.

MRS. JENKINS: And the men?

PAUL: No! I'm—

MRS. JENKINS: *Paul*. I'm *kidding*.

PAUL: Okay.

MRS. JENKINS: You're as serious as cancer. (*beat*) Don't read the bible. Please.

PAUL: I want to know.

MRS. JENKINS: Is it that you want to know, or is it that you want to stay in the good graces of those two girls.

PAUL: Um...

MRS. JENKINS: Amanda and Jill. They're cute. But not for you.

PAUL: How do you know they're not for me?

MRS. JENKINS: Their *religion*, Paul.

PAUL: That's not...

MRS. JENKINS: It *is* a factor. Such a factor. You'll find you can't get in. Not really.

PAUL: Anyone can get in. It's easy.

MRS. JENKINS: But is that what you really want to do? You're about to go to a college that is literally *on the ocean*. Think of the girls who'll be there, Paul.

PAUL: I have trouble picturing that. Them. I know they're waiting but.

MRS. JENKINS: But you have a history with Amanda and Jill.

PAUL: More Amanda than Jill. But Jill...

MRS. JENKINS: You see her as special. Because you think she's attainable.

Silence.

MRS. JENKINS: Why do you have no self-confidence, Paul.

PAUL: I...

MRS. JENKINS: None whatsoever. You're a sponge that soaks up the favors of everyone around you.

Silence.

PAUL: I suppose...it's my dad...

MRS. JENKINS: He's gone now. You're free. (*pause*) I am sorry for your loss, but you are free. I know what he did to you over the years. Brad told me. Your dad wasn't the Badger—

PAUL: But he had his demons. (*pause*) I wonder what the end was like for him, I don't mean his physical death but his spiritual...If he crossed over or...

MRS. JENKINS: Or if it's all a lie and when it happens your world goes black and that's it, lights out.

PAUL: I want to know. I want some kind of control.

MRS. JENKINS: What you want is to keep those girls, one or both of them, in your life. You want to control *them*. That's not a reason to become one of them. In my opinion.

Silence.

MRS. JENKINS: You remind me of me, Paul.

PAUL: That's not possible.

MRS. JENKINS: But it is.

PAUL: Is it because of your lack of confidence? Because of the Badger? I mean here you are, this A.P. Lit teacher at Anomar High, for Christ's sake, and you're with this—you were with this...this WWF-watching beer guzzling big-bellied *trash heap*.

MRS. JENKINS: Time for me to go now. I've certainly sobered up.

PAUL: You had to have known. What he was doing to Brad. And Tyler. You must've. You're not blind.

MRS. JENKINS: Careful, Paul.

PAUL: I swear if you knew—

MRS. JENKINS: *I didn't know!*

PAUL: You chose not to know. With as much abuse as Brad and Tyler put up with.

Mrs. Jenkins takes a deep breath.

MRS. JENKINS: We are done talking, Paul.

PAUL: At least he wasn't Brad's real father—

MRS. JENKINS: Don't go *any* further. (*pause*) Maybe you do need to find religion, Paul.

Mrs. Jenkins puts the cigarettes in her purse and turns to leave.

PAUL: Princess Diana died tonight.

MRS. JENKINS: I heard. (*pause*) Good night, Paul. Please don't suffer the little children too much on your road to Damascus.

Mrs. Jenkins exits. Sound of the buzzer and sliding doors. Silence except for the faint music overhead. Lights down and the same spot on Paul—and the same undoing of the tie and unbuttoning of the shirt—as before.

PAUL: The road to Damascus. Suffer the little children unto me. My senior year I started reading that good book, along with whatever Mrs. Jenkins assigned in A.P. I did it for Brad, what we talked about that last day of his life. The New Testament alongside Kafka, Camus, Conrad, Beckett. Mrs. J had never taught some of those before. *The Trial. Waiting for Godot. The Stranger.* She told me she felt compelled to throw existentialism our way, after what happened to Brad. Why are we here? What's the point? Bigger than the bomb. At times I felt I was losing my mind. I knew I had to go to college, there was no other choice, it's just what we did then. I knew of no other options, and then, as I read the chapters and verses, Revelation, a seed of an option planted itself in my mind. It was there, not yet ready to sprout. I kept it safe as I got through my senior year focused, determined not to lose them, either of them. I played it safe with Amanda, we went on dates, unchaperoned knowing nothing would happen. I didn't see her that way. I never thought she might want me to see her that way. But Jill: the outsider. I could have her, if I only knew her. I had this idea that I could learn everything about her, and that she would come. I was consumed by fantasies, not all of which were right. Would she slide through her window after her family had gone to sleep, or would she get her brother to drive her over, then get him to stay and watch us, make sure nothing happened that we wanted to happen?

Mom worried about Jill. But why? I wondered. What's the big deal? So what if she's a Saint?

Mom saw it coming. Our first date was the two of us in the front of the car and two of Jill's friends in the back. I wasn't expecting to be chaperoned—on that or any of the other dates we went on. And why would I when Amanda, who was far more religious, didn't bring along anyone? Was it because they saw me as safe, vanilla, a friend only? These thoughts infuriated me. And Mom expressing her distaste for Jill and Amanda's religion, that old and new prejudice. But did she know how much I didn't care? How much I needed to be with Jill after that kiss, that first kiss? In Jill I saw my future. And yet...It's so cold in here, and lonely.

Jill knew where I was that night, both those nights that last weekend in August. It's not so long ago, and she knew. She knew we'd be leaving for different colleges in less than two weeks.

Eleven at night to seven in the morning. Eight hours. Eight hours in which to stop by. She assured me she would. And I couldn't wait.

SCENE 3

Around 3:30 in the morning. Paul, on the stool, slumps a bit, fighting to stay awake. He closes his eyes for just a moment that turns into a longer moment...Sound of the buzzer and the doors sliding open. Groggy, Paul stands up and gets behind the register. TOM and IAN, guys Paul knows from high school, walk in.

TOM: What you want, Ian?

IAN: Ho-Hos. They got Ho-Hos here?

TOM: I don't know. Let's ask....Prell—that you? Yeah, fuck yeah it is. Hey, Ian, Prell's working here.

IAN: Course, fool. I've seen him around. I told you that.

TOM: Prell, you got any Ho-Hos?

PAUL: On the rack to your right.

TOM: There's just bread here, man.

PAUL: Oh, sorry. I mean my right...that'd be your left.

Tom helps Ian pick out the Ho-Hos. He then pushes Ian over to the register.

TOM: Pay this guy, Ian.

IAN: Thought you were gonna spot me.

TOM: Spot yourself this time. Bank O' Tom is closed Sundays at 3:30 am. How you like graveyard shift, Prell?

PAUL: It's all right.

TOM: Yeah? It sucks already and I'm standing on the other side of the counter. How many times have you been doing this?

PAUL: Uh, this is my second night. First time, second night.

IAN: A graveyard virgin.

PAUL: I guess so.

TOM: Aren't you going to college, Prell?

PAUL: Yeah. I'm giving them my two week's notice on Monday, actually.

TOM: Prell, you should just quit.

IAN: Quit now. Right the fuck now!

TOM: None of this two week's bullshit. Just up and leave the store. Tonight. This morning I mean.

IAN: With us.

TOM: You sure about that, Ian? (*to Paul*) We've got some real good shit in the car. The trunk, to be safe. You could smoke out with us.

IAN: Yeah, smoke out with us.

PAUL: Um, I'm not—I...No thanks, guys.

TOM: Not that I was expecting anything different from you. But I had to try.

PAUL: Thanks. (*beat*) Hey, you guys hear about Diana?

TOM: Princess Di, sure.

IAN: 'Course. We don't live under rocks.

PAUL: Pretty terrible, huh.

TOM: S'pose so. TV seems to think so. Can't change a channel without seeing some poor sad-ass crying about her. Makes me want to re-up early. I'm gonna need the extra stash to get through all the worldwide weeping. This is just the start, Prell. It all changes after tonight.

PAUL: What does?

IAN: Everything. You heard the man.

TOM: Everything.

IAN: So I'm taking these Ho-Hos.

TOM: You're buying 'em.

Ian takes out his wallet.

IAN: Lemme see your wallet, Prell.

PAUL: What? No.

TOM: C'mon. He's not gonna rob you or anything. He just wants to see it. (*pause*) What, you got porn pics of Princess Di in there or what?

Paul pulls out his wallet but doesn't hand it over.

IAN: Lemme see your prom pictures.

PAUL: I...don't have any.

IAN: Liar. Everyone's got prom pictures in their wallet. Everyone. Lemme see 'em.

PAUL: Why?

IAN: 'Cause it's a special occasion and I'm interested, that's all. Shit. Can you believe this guy? Must have Di's left nipple in there!

TOM: Or your mom.

IAN: Or his mom.

Tom and Ian high-five as they laugh wildly. Reluctantly, Paul opens his wallet and flips through the pictures inside. Ian places a finger on one of the photos.

IAN: Jill, huh.

TOM: Yeah. You know her?

IAN: I've seen her around. You take her to prom?

PAUL: Uh, no. I took Amanda.

IAN: Amanda *Holm*? Where's your prom photo?

PAUL: It's...here.

IAN: *Behind* Jill. Damn. Bet you really wanted to take her instead.

PAUL: You could say that.

IAN: I *did* say that. How blue were your balls, Prell?

PAUL: *What?*

IAN: No way you got laid on prom night, right?

PAUL: Uh...We kissed.

IAN: Oh shit, Prell. I got my mom for kissing. But I understand. I see. Amanda's cute. Jill's not bad too. She's hot in a kinky sort of way.

Tom looks at Jill's picture.

TOM: I'd do her.

IAN: Good luck, mo-fo. You a Saint?

TOM: She's one of them? I didn't know that.

IAN: Man, half this town is them. Amanda and Jill... Prell's making the rounds. You weren't always one, were you, Prell? When did you convert?

PAUL: I'm not a Saint.

IAN: Whuh. Really?

PAUL: No. Why would you think that?

Ian laughs.

IAN: Look at yourself, Prell!

PAUL: What, I'm not in her religion.

IAN: Then why the fuck you take a Saint girl to prom? Why the fuck you hung up on another one now?

PAUL: Because.

IAN: Because...You like not getting laid.

PAUL: She's not devout. She's really rebellious, actually.

IAN: Shit, Prell. That solves *everything*.

PAUL: Look, guys...

IAN: Look, *Prell*. I been there.

TOM: When did you go for a Saint?

IAN: A while back, that's all.

TOM: Who?

IAN: Think I'm telling you? Here. Have a Ho-Ho.

PAUL: She's coming over here pretty soon.

IAN: Jill? Oh shit, Prell. Good thing you got plenty of condoms in this place.

TOM: Want us to put a sign over the door?

PAUL: Uh, that's okay.

TOM: We'll be seeing you, Prell.

PAUL: Yeah, sure.

IAN: Stay away from 'em is my advice. That's a dead end road, unless you join. They'll drop you, Prell.

PAUL: Yeah right.

IAN: I bet they're talking about it now. Yeah, they'll drop you like a rock.

PAUL: We've known each other since—

IAN: And you really think that matters to 'em, when you're not one of 'em? Shit, Prell. Wake up. This is *your* life.

TOM: Your mom.

IAN: Tom, what the fuck.

TOM: His mom.

IAN: Whatever. See you around, Prell.

Tom and Ian exit. Lights down and spot on Paul, as before.

PAUL: Start of summer after my sophomore year I decided to write a screenplay. I wrote it in a week. I was sixteen. The title: *Frankenhunk*. You can guess what it was about. Was it any good? My friends seemed to think so. We were just teens driving around that summer with a couple camcorders and old clothes found at the thrift store on Main Street. We didn't really know what we were doing, we only knew we had nothing else to do and this was fun. I cast everyone I could. Brad was Frankenhunk's monster, I was the inventor, Amanda was the love interest. Jill wouldn't have a role until the sequel, *Bride of Frankenhunk*, filmed that fall.

I remember feeling good that summer, in my car, driving my friends around, directing them, messing around with the props, the costumes, the music we dubbed in later. That first film was so bad and so special...My high couldn't last, though, not when my parents were my parents. They found out I'd been driving people when I wasn't supposed to. The insurance, the rules. They blew up on me, my father especially. That afternoon was bad. I thought then of the summer of '95 as the Bloody Summer. I was sixteen, remember, and thought too much of myself, not enough of my father. I hated him then. I saw him only as an obstacle to my fantasies of becoming the next Tarantino. We'd never been close, and now this.

But I finished it. *Frankenhunk*, at least among the students at Anomar High, the cast members and their friends, was a hit, and I vowed to make more. I thought I knew my path then. Toward the end of my senior year, two films under my belt and a third in the works, I was assured I'd be attending a college in LA renowned for its film program. I was all set. And then...the hike, my father's fall. After the funeral in June I got back to work on that third film that I couldn't yet admit was going nowhere. Why was I still at it when most all of my friends had moved on? Jill. I wanted to film her. She was the protagonist. I thought about her constantly. It took a lot for me not to put my fantasies out there on film. She thought it strange she was pretty much the only cast member, the two of us, my Annie Hall. I didn't see a problem with it. We had developed, I thought, into a couple over the past several months despite the fact I'd taken Amanda to both homecoming and prom. That hurt Jill, but she stayed with me. She too lacked so much confidence.

The day I came over to her house, Pioneer Day, the 150th anniversary, and I turned my camera on, which in turn turned me on. Of course I wanted sex, and I wanted it with her. The playfulness we engaged in that day her family was gone demonstrated a tension I realize scared Jill—and scared her off. At the end I still had hope. I was on the phone with her the Thursday before my weekend graveyard shift, and we were talking the way we used to, back before I panicked and got insistent. I wasn't insistent about working graveyard but I was lonely, and she agreed to come keep me company. We were about to leave our little town, and it really was okay if nothing big happened, really, she was a Saint and I was just as scared of sex as she was. But the last thing she said to me was "I'll be there." "When?" I said. "Before your Saturday shift is over." She said it could be night or morning, beginning or end, but she would be there.

Mom liked to get the last word in. She liked to get the last anything in, actually. A typical argument would often escalate and end with me leaving the room. I did start to leave the room after telling her I was for sure working the graveyard shift at the gas station. This was right after my phone call with Jill and I still had her in my mind, strong. "You have my permission to quit, Paul," Mom said. She also said, "Age has nothing to do with it. It's a matter of safety. I don't feel safe when you're alone at a gas station from night until morning." Of course I wasn't thinking when I blurted out I wouldn't be alone, someone special was coming to see me. "Who, that Saint girl," she said. "Her name's Jill," I said, and I turned my back, but Mom froze me with what she said next: "You can't make somebody love you." (*beat*) For a while I believed that. And then I thought of Jill and Amanda, their religion, all that I'd read and learned so far and would continue to learn. And I thought, You're wrong, Mom. You *can* make somebody love you. You most certainly can.

SCENE 4

Six-thirty in the morning and the place is packed. Customers mill about in the background, many trying to get an acceptable cup of coffee from the canisters that aren't giving anything. A lot of grumbling and rising murmurs. A line has formed at the counter, behind which stands a haggard and dejected Paul. He rings up customers as quickly as possible, but the line doesn't want to show its tail. The sliding doors buzz off-stage and in walks Paul's coworker TRISH, dressed in the standard-issue company shirt, striped tie and black dress shorts. Right away she has a hard look about her: she goes over to the coffee pots and canisters and checks them as customers continue to complain. In a buff Trish finally approaches Paul. She gets in his face using her pointer finger.

TRISH: What happened to the coffee?

PAUL: I didn't change it.

TRISH: *Obviously*. You're supposed to make it fresh every hour starting at four.

PAUL: Yeah, well, I got busy. I'm busy now so...

Trish leaves for other areas of the store. As Paul cuts the line down to only a few customers, his coworker can be seen in the background inspecting the rows, the shelves, etc. Paul sends the last of the customers on their way and Trish returns to his side.

TRISH: Do you even remember how to close out?

PAUL: Of course. I did it yesterday. You were here, *remember?*

TRISH: Then how come this place isn't sweeped? You did it Friday. (*pause*) And it's dirty over there. That's not passable by this store's standards. Keith's going to have a shit-fit about the shelves...all these mistakes...I can't believe you. What changed between this shift and your last one?

PAUL: I'll tell you what changed: the world. The whole god-damned world changed overnight. And you wanna know why? Because she's dead. Crushed in a car, photographed by the papa—the papa...the papa-whatever. Her and her boyfriend and their bodyguard and her dreams and her face and breasts and her body and her relief work for the little African children and her royal crown and her accent and her nose and her glare and her pantsuits and her money and her misty mountain top and her earrings and her handshakes and her newly discovered land mines and her photo opportunities and her face, her face on every magazine, every page, her face. And I don't know what's going to happen from now on. I really don't. That's what's changed. I don't.

TRISH (*beat*): Are you talking about Princess Diana?

PAUL: I'm talking about someone I thought was special to me. I thought anyway.

TRISH: What are you going on about?

PAUL: I can have it both ways. Vengeance is mine. I just have to read.

Paul takes off his tie and starts unbuttoning his work shirt.

PAUL: Tell Keith I'm going to college. And I'm keeping the uniform.

Paul downs the last of his soda, throws the cup in a nearby trashcan, and heads out.

TRISH: You can't go. You haven't closed out yet!

PAUL: I'm just full of surprises, aren't I?

TRISH: Get back here and close out!

Lights down, spot on Paul, who sits on the edge of the stage.

PAUL: I called her something terrible in the car, a slur I'd never use now that I'm on a new path. That slur was not just for her, though. That day I started down my path. (*pause*) I could still feel her breath on my neck, her lips almost against mine. I jumped in the driver's seat and slammed the door shut, feeling like that driver as he entered the tunnel. This is the future, right. I started the engine and shifted into first. No, I needed to go in reverse. That is unless I wanted to crash through the front of the store, which seemed about right just then. All I wanted was bed and covers thrown over me, a message from Jill—my Jill, my faith—saying she was sorry, she'd meant to come at seven when my shift was over Sunday so we could go to breakfast together, dance on the tables, pour syrup down each other's throats, but her mom made her go to church and rather than leave on bad footing she went. (*pause*) I did not want to see myself in the rearview mirror, so I kept my eyes on the yellow lines instead. I was home just after seven. Mom was on the couch, her eyes on me instead of the TV. I passed by with a nod and a feeble wave. "How'd it go?" she said. I mumbled something unintelligible and swayed down the hall. The blinds were drawn, the room dark and cool. I slid under the covers and thought about all that had happened since I met her, the reasons why she would never see me again. I was awake when the door to my room opened softly. My eyes shut, my lips parted slightly, I sensed a female presence reach out. She bent down and hugged me fiercely, seeming not to care if I was conscious or not. She kissed me on the cheek, then withdrew without a word. The door shut and I lay there on my side. "Mom," I said as my morning turned into night.

Slow fade to darkness.

MERIBAH

TIME: August 1996

PLACE: The San Diego Country Gems, a hilly and isolated suburban enclave near the town of Anomar, approximately forty miles northeast inland from the city of San Diego.

SETTING: The backyard of Paul's house. In the center is a small square patch of lawn and on all sides of that is gravel. In the b.g.: some fruit trees and a short wooden fence.

CAST:

Paul, 18
Brad, 17
Amanda, 16
Alex, 19

Meribah

PAUL lies on the grassy lawn reading a book and listening to something on his Walkman. He wears shorts, a t-shirt and sunglasses. After a few moments, he notices someone climbing over the fence off-stage. Paul marks his book, sets it down, takes off his headphones and pauses the Walkman. He looks up to see BRAD enter. Brad, like Paul, is wearing a simple t-shirt and shorts (all black as opposed to Paul's white and beige combo). Unlike Paul, he is not wearing sunglasses, and he is also carrying a long samurai sword. Brad crosses the gravel and approaches Paul. He stabs the sword into the lawn so that it stands hilt-up.

BRAD: My liege.

PAUL: I didn't know there was another renaissance faire. I would've gone.

BRAD: No renaissance faire.

PAUL: What's with your sword then? I thought you never took it down.

Brad sits down next to Paul.

BRAD: What are you listening to?

PAUL: "Thick as a Brick."

BRAD: Awesome song, awesome. I can't believe a kid wrote it.

PAUL: Well he didn't write the song, he—

BRAD: He wrote the poem, I know.

PAUL: Poem. Right. (*pause*) Sorry.

BRAD: No worries. He's a genius...

PAUL: Sure is. He's probably dead, I think.

BRAD: You think?

PAUL: Well I mean how come we've never heard of him? If he was still alive, and he was ten in, what, 1972, maybe 1971, that would make him....

BRAD: Thirty-five. Or thirty-four, depending.

PAUL: Yeah, so if he's such a genius with this "Thick as a Brick" poem, don't you think he would have amassed this amazing...I don't know, repertoire by now?

BRAD: Maybe he's only known in England.

PAUL: Yeah. I sometimes forget this is British, isn't it? But you'd think we would have heard something about him in some magazine or newspaper, you know. (*pause*) I doubt this would be his only successful poem.

BRAD: Maybe he flamed out.

PAUL: Yeah?

BRAD: Maybe he got into some hardcore drugs.

PAUL: At age ten?

BRAD: In his teen years. Remember Drew Barrymore—

PAUL: True. But I bet one of two things: one, that he's still alive and he's flying under the radar, publishing these little books of poems in England...

BRAD: With even more bands than Jethro Tull turning his words into music.

PAUL: Exactly. Or two: he's dead, and he died really young, probably of some terrible disease like child leukemia or something.

BRAD: I hope not.

PAUL: Yeah. That would bite. Talk about a talent wasted. But I hate to say it: I think two is what happened. I think he probably died right after he won this big prize for the poem, and then Jethro Tull set the poem to music with his parents' permission.

BRAD: Pretty cool parents.

PAUL: Yeah, pretty cool.

Silence.

BRAD: Whatcha reading?

PAUL: Kafka. Letter to his father. I just started. It's great. Really goes well with "Thick as a Brick." Reading Kafka's letter to his father, listening to "Thick as a Brick"...great combo.

BRAD: They really go well together, huh.

PAUL: They do.

Paul takes up the liner notes to the CD case lying next to the Walkman. He flips through the thin booklet.

PAUL: They really connect, and what's more: they connect to my own life.

Brad takes the liner notes from Paul.

BRAD: Dude, you underlined the whole song!

PAUL: Not the whole song. Just the parts that spoke to me.

BRAD: It's not English class, Paul.

PAUL: I know. But still.

BRAD: You'll be ready for my mom, anyway.

Silence. Paul takes off his sunglasses and gnaws on one of the ends.

PAUL: Did you, uh, did you get a chance to read the script?

BRAD (*carefully*): I did.

PAUL: What did you think?

BRAD (*pause*): I don't know, Paul. It wasn't...like the other two.

PAUL: Oh.

BRAD: Don't take it personally.

PAUL: I'm not. I won't.

BRAD: I think it's time for Frankenhunk to die.

PAUL (*feigning despair*): No! Not Frankenhunk! (*pause*) You seriously think I shouldn't do this?

BRAD: Do another movie. Don't do another *Frankenhunk*. I'll star in anything, but...those movies were kinda for when we were younger. Now that we're seniors...

PAUL: I have to make something more mature.

BRAD: Doesn't have to be adult. Just: different from what you've already done. You don't want to get into a rut, man.

PAUL (*pause*): Well. Okay.

BRAD: See. You're pissed off.

PAUL: I am not.

BRAD: You totally are!

PAUL: Whatever.

BRAD: Yeah. Whatever.

Silence.

PAUL: Did you, um, did you get thrown out?

BRAD (*eyes on liner notes*): Nah. I threw him out.

PAUL: Holy shit. Really? What happened? Is that why...

Paul gestures to the sword.

BRAD: I used it.

PAUL: Uh. How?

BRAD: I had to use it. He forced my hand.

PAUL: He went after you.

BRAD: Not after me. After Tyler.

PAUL: Jesus.

BRAD: Today was the breaking point. I'd had enough. *We'd* had enough.

PAUL: That bad, huh.

BRAD: That's putting it lightly.

PAUL: I didn't mean—

BRAD: It's okay. You never knew just how bad it was. Pretty much constant, daily, but never anything major, nothing that'd send us to the hospital or anything like that. Just little things, like pushing me or Ty into a wall, like in the hallway most times.

PAUL: I knew he was abusive...

BRAD: We'd pass him in the hall and he'd push us and say things like, Oops, didn't see ya there, and other times he wouldn't say a word. He acted like it was nothing. He wanted it to be nothing. He warned us not to leave any marks on the wall. But he was just as worried about us having marks on our bodies. So whatever he did, he did just enough so it didn't leave a mark. Pretty much anything that didn't leave a mark—there were words, sure, but when he got physical he always made sure not to leave any evidence.

PAUL: I knew it.

BRAD: So like bending the fingers back—

PAUL: Jesus!

BRAD: —in the bathroom, sure. Or just shoving. He'd shove a lot. We had to get out of his way.

PAUL: That bastard.

BRAD: More than a bastard.

PAUL: Man. Why is your mom with him? She's been with him a long time. And she's an English teacher, teaching A.P., and she's with *that* guy?

BRAD: I don't know. It's the great secret of my mom's life, I guess. I knew Amelia was really wild when she was younger, I think she hung out with a lot of guys like Badger, these motorcycle guys who play guitar and sing, and they were going to do an album together.

PAUL: An album?

BRAD: Yeah. Like she'd write the lyrics and he'd do the music. It never got off the ground.

PAUL: So he can't get his act together so he takes it out on you.

BRAD: But it wasn't going to happen this time. Not after today. I heard him in the living room, pushing Tyler around this morning. Not this time, I thought. He'd do it more to Ty just because he's younger, and I felt, for the first time really, I felt this morning I could really do something. I had to help him —I'd gone too long not doing anything. I thought of that framed picture of my stepfather playing his fucking guitar with a toothpick in his mouth..."Badger Plays the Blues." How much I wanted to smash that with my fist, smash him somehow. For what he was doing to my brother. Ty was getting the worst of it. I had my door closed and the music on loud but it didn't matter, he might as well have been beating up my brother in my room. I concentrated on the banging and the thumping. It didn't sound like the wall anymore. When I heard Tyler cry out I snapped, this red burst, like a rose, blossomed in front of me, I smelled something hot and I went to my wall where I kept the sword. Hung there, perfect balance. I grabbed the sword and drew it out of its sheath. It wasn't sharp but it would do. I couldn't see accurately, even a few feet in front of me and I was so scared I would miss, that he would kill me and this uprising would fail. But it wouldn't. Not this time. I threw open my door and ran down the hall, past "Badger Plays the Blues," past that, screaming like a little kid. The sword was straight out in front of me and anyone who came out of a room right then would've got skewered. I ran into the living room where I saw him half-shoving, half-sucker punching Ty, just little punches, nothing that would send us to the hospital or even to Amelia. I don't know what I was saying but I think it was another, a new language, brought out in a roar. There was only him and the sword then. He thought I was joking at first. He looked at the sword and laughed a little. I drove it at his big bloated belly, at the goddess tattoo. The tip cut him on the side and drew blood. He kind of gasped and looked at me with what I'd never seen in him before: fear. Fear made his eyes bluer than ever. And he kept saying, What the fuck, what the fuck, Bradley, what the fuck, you sick little psycho. And I said, Get out of our fucking house, get out! Leave! Forever! I mean it! I raised the sword and prepared to swing. He saw I was serious. I was going to kill him. I would have. But he ran. He took off across the living room, knocked the lamp off the table on his way out. I ran him right out the front door. And I kept following him, crying and screaming and laughing at how weak he always was—it just took someone to stand up to him. I went after him, in the sun, the heat, the music still blaring in my head, and I followed him down the road, cutting into his presence, cutting into the past, cutting, and when I got back to the house Amelia held me tight and said You did the right thing.

Silence.

PAUL: Wow. I mean. That happened this morning.

Brad nods, stares at the sword.

PAUL: So...he's gone. (*pause*) No more Badger.

BRAD: No more Badge of Horror.

PAUL: I can't believe it. I've known him for so long. Eight years...

BRAD: But you didn't know him. I didn't know him. My brother didn't know him.

PAUL: Okay.

BRAD: He was just a man.

PAUL: A monster.

BRAD: A man with a can of Spam.

PAUL: A monster with a can—

BRAD: Don't say monster!

Silence.

BRAD (*a confiding tone*): You see, Paul, if you say monster it makes him more than what he is. I don't want that. You don't either. You don't have to live with him.

PAUL: I sure felt like I was living with him, whenever I was at your house.

BRAD: Yeah...

PAUL: The dinners with him just watching me with those iced-over eyes, his mouth working behind that long nasty beard...

BRAD: Right.

PAUL: And the times he'd come by the room...that one time he saw us playing action figures, and he looked at us like...

BRAD: It was bad, I know.

PAUL: The guy would yell at me on the phone if I didn't call between a certain time and a certain time. And the times always changed!

BRAD: But that's just it: he's just some guy, some guy Amelia met in a bar in Dallas, who followed her out here, and who would help support her and us whenever he was able to work. When he did get work, it was good for us because he got so much money. But construction's not constant, and so we were either with a lot of money or hardly any money.

PAUL: I still don't know what she saw in him.

BRAD: You'll never know. I won't either. It's something I know not to talk about with her. (*beat*) I think she's ashamed.

PAUL: Isn't she, like, the head of the English department? And she chose a guy who didn't read.

BRAD: Oh, Badger read. He didn't read much, but he read. (*beat*) Opposites attract, man.

PAUL: I guess. I just can't believe, with how smart your mom is, she didn't see—

BRAD: Hey! She didn't, Paul. She didn't, and that's all there is to it.

PAUL: Okay. Okay. (*pause*) So no more Moloch.

BRAD: Moloch?

PAUL: It's in the Bible, the Old Testament.

BRAD: *You're* reading *the Bible*?

PAUL: Sure. You told me you're reading the dictionary, front to back.

BRAD: There's a pretty big difference, Paul.

PAUL: But both are mad quests.

BRAD: I'm gonna do it. I'm on 'D' now.

PAUL: You got through 'A,' B,' and 'C'? Seriously?

BRAD: Totally.

PAUL: I better step up my reading then. I'm just kind of skipping around.

BRAD: And you landed on Moloch.

PAUL: Yeah, Moloch. This Old Testament Hebrew deity that parents supposedly sacrificed their children to.

BRAD: Isn't that just the story of Isaac or something?

PAUL: Kind of, but on a much more frequent scale, I think. It's like Moloch always has to have a child sacrifice, so parents were always burning their kids up on the altar.

BRAD: Sounds fun.

PAUL: If you were a parent.

BRAD: But then you gotta wonder how did the population survive?

PAUL: Oh, it was only a certain group of people that worshipped Moloch, I think. And so they must've died out, eventually.

BRAD: You're saying Amelia sacrificed me and Tyler to the Badger, our Moloch?

PAUL (*beat*): No...

BRAD: That's what you're saying. You said, "So no more Moloch." Did you or did you not say that?

PAUL (*pause*): I did say that. I'm sorry. (*pause*) I'm really sorry, Brad. I didn't mean—

BRAD: I know. You're you.

Silence.

PAUL: Do you think he'll come back?

BRAD: I helped Amelia and Tyler put all his stuff out in the driveway before I left. Even the motorcycles. He'll probably come back tonight, but he's not getting in—not when I'm there. He can get his stuff and go.

PAUL: How long was he in your life?

BRAD: Ten years. Longest I think Amelia's been with any guy. (*pause*) Mom says we're moving.

PAUL: Moving? You mean...

BRAD: Not out of the Gems. Just to another house—it'll probably be even closer to you.

PAUL: Oh, well...

BRAD: I'm probably going to need a ride to school, when it starts, if that's okay.

PAUL: That's fine. I understand.

BRAD: He's not going to be able to find us, after we move.

PAUL: I'm sure he won't. That's...great, Brad. (*pause*) Why'd you, uh, why'd you bring the sword over here then—if you were done with it, I mean.

BRAD: I'm not done with it.

PAUL: Okay...

BRAD: I wanted to show you what you've been missing.

PAUL: I've seen the sword, man.

BRAD: It's what the sword represents: power, freedom, strength—all the things you're missing.

PAUL: I'm missing them? What do you mean?

BRAD: Wake up, Paul. Man, you gotta wake up!

PAUL (*beat*): Brad. Are you on something right now?

BRAD: Actually, I am.

Brad takes out a little plastic baggy. In it are what look to be a few pills.

PAUL: What the fuck, Brad!

BRAD: Shhhh...

PAUL: You have drugs in my backyard?

BRAD: It's not like anyone's gonna see.

PAUL: Are those...pills?

BRAD: Ecstasy.

PAUL: What?

BRAD: E. You know.

PAUL: Um, I don't know, actually.

BRAD: C'mon, Paul. You've heard of E. It's the thing I was telling you about at the beginning of this summer—you know at the diner...

PAUL: Oh, yeah. I kind of blocked that out.

BRAD: Well block it back in.

Brad pushes a pill on Paul, who refuses.

PAUL: Dude, what are you thinking? Didn't you know I didn't want to do it back then, and now I'm in my backyard, in broad daylight, with my parents coming home any minute, and you think I'll want to do it now?

BRAD: No. I didn't think you'd want to do it. But I thought I could convince you.

PAUL: Some way to convince me.

BRAD: Paul. Why are you not cool?

PAUL: Huh?

BRAD: I mean you're still my friend, but it's kind of like we're only friends because we say we're friends, not because we actually do anything that friends do.

PAUL: What, like do drugs together? Is this why you've been avoiding me all summer, not calling me back, ever since I said I wouldn't go with you and everyone else down to La Jolla and do this stuff on the beach? Is that it?

BRAD: That *is* fucking it, if you really want to know.

PAUL: I do really want to know. I've been hurt—

BRAD: Oh *you've* been hurt? That's hilarious, Paul. Really a cut-up there.

PAUL: Yeah. I thought we were friends.

BRAD: We are friends. At least, we can be again.

Brad offers the pill.

PAUL: This is a far cry from the Golden Egg.

BRAD (*nostalgic*): The Golden Egg...

PAUL: What does it, um, what does this do?

Paul takes the pill and inspects it.

BRAD: It's kind of like—here's my theory, okay. It's kind of like we fucked up, and we know we fucked up ever since the Garden of Eden, Paradise, when God threw our asses out. We had paradise, and we lost it. And so everything we've been doing—all the hurt we've been giving each other, all the emotion, all the shit—all that's been our way of trying to get back to where we once were. And now we've found the ultimate way to get back. (*pause*) This stuff, Paul, E is amazing. It's going to make you feel so good...you're going to not care, you're going to finally loosen up, and...you're going to finally get laid.

PAUL: What, with you? (*pause*) Have you gotten laid?

Brad smiles. Silence.

PAUL: With who?

BRAD: Let's just say you know her.

PAUL: Who, Becky?

Brad shakes his head.

PAUL: Christina?

Brad doesn't shake his head. He smiles coyly and looks at the grass.

PAUL: No way. Christy? Jesus. That's—

BRAD: It was fucking awesome. Paul, you can't believe how good it feels. To lose it with this other person, to just lose control for a while, it's the greatest thing in the world.

PAUL: And she was on this too?

BRAD: That's what La Jolla Cove is for.

PAUL: I'll be damned.

BRAD: There's a little cave on the beach, close to where we park—

PAUL: Okay. I mean, spare me the details, please. (*pause*) Everyone else was there?

BRAD: Not in the cave, but they were there.

Silence.

BRAD: So today's a test run. A celebration for what happened this morning. A bunch of us are going to the beach on Friday. You gotta be there this time.

Paul considers the pill in his hand.

PAUL: It really makes you feel that good, huh.

BRAD: Like you can do anything.

PAUL: It doesn't fuck you up when you have sex?

BRAD: It makes you want to be with anyone, anytime, anywhere. Way better than alcohol.

Silence.

PAUL: Let me just ask you, Brad: Why do you need this?

Brad laughs harshly.

BRAD: It's gotta be obvious.

PAUL (*pause*): Okay, it is. But so maybe that question's for me. Why do *I* need this?

BRAD: Because if you don't, Paul...

PAUL: What'll happen?

BRAD: I just see you alone, years from now. I don't want you to be alone.

PAUL: I won't be alone. Not when I have—

BRAD: You're thinking too much about things again.

PAUL: But see that's my nature—just as it's your nurture.

BRAD: What do you mean?

PAUL: Do I need this? I'm going to college. I have a lot of things going for me. I have to start getting the applications together—

BRAD: Paul—

PAUL: Gotta finish reading the books for A.P.—

BRAD: You—

PAUL: Your mom wants us to write something before—

BRAD: Paul! You judgmental fuck! Why do you hate me?

PAUL: I don't—

BRAD: Yes you do! Liar. You look down on me like no one else—and you're my "friend." Whatever that means.

Silence. Paul hangs his head, yanks at the grass.

BRAD: What does it mean to you? Because you know I don't really know. Are friends just people to you? People you know you can get rid of any time? I'd like to say you can't get rid of me, but I'm thinking now it's me who needs to get rid of you. And that I can do easily.

PAUL: Brad.

BRAD: I try. I invited you places at the start of summer—

PAUL: Brad. Come—

BRAD: But. I can't keep trying. Not when you judge me: "Oh, Brad. He comes from a broken home, never knew his father, his mom chooses losers even though she teaches A.P. Lit at the high school, a walking contradiction. Brad had to uproot his life in Texas—"

PAUL: I moved too—

BRAD: "...his stepfather's a drunken motorcycle-riding WWF-watching monster, and his mom's a chain-smoking heavy drinker—"

PAUL: She drinks?

BRAD: "Brad's family isn't like mine. My parents were college sweethearts, they've been together forever." But not everyone stays together, Paul. Some people are only together for a night.

PAUL: I had no idea you felt this way about me.

BRAD: For a while now, yeah.

PAUL: You really think I judge you?

BRAD: I know you do. My new friends, I know you judge them too. When are you going to see, man?

Silence.

PAUL: You didn't tell me any of this.

BRAD: I'm telling you now. I wanted to tell you when you got rid of the Nintendo.

PAUL: The Nintendo!

Paul laughs sharply.

PAUL: I knew you were upset about that.

BRAD: You're too good for video games now.

PAUL: I sold it all—I sold everything—because I made a decision to change my life, get serious about things. You gotta leave the kid stuff behind, man. I mean seriously, right? I have, and I'm happy.

BRAD: I believe you about the seriousness—totally—but not about the happiness.

PAUL: What do you really know about happiness?

BRAD: I know this.

Brad indicates the pill in his own palm.

BRAD: Together.

PAUL: I don't think so.

Paul looks around the yard, the pill clenched.

BRAD: If you throw it I'm gonna start swinging—and I don't mean my fists.

PAUL: Oh yeah?

BRAD: Oh yeah.

AMANDA enters. She wears sandals and a long dress. Upon seeing her, Paul quickly hides his pill. Brad is less hesitant to do so.

AMANDA: Oh hi, Brad. (*to Paul*): I knocked on the door and rang the bell but—

PAUL: Sorry. I forgot.

AMANDA: It's okay. You're joining us, Brad?

BRAD: Joining you for what?

AMANDA: I guess not.

BRAD: You look hot.

AMANDA: Oh. Um. You mean...

BRAD: I mean that dress doesn't look comfortable out here.

AMANDA: It's a sundress.

Brad shrugs.

AMANDA: It's...not ideal. Out here.

BRAD: So wear shorts?

AMANDA: My mom would quite literally freak out.

BRAD: I'm sorry.

AMANDA: That's how it is. I don't mind. It's not that bad out.

PAUL: I'm glad you showed up. I think I got a burn.

AMANDA: Have you been reading for A.P., Brad?

BRAD: I still have a week.

AMANDA: You haven't started? (*beat*) Does your mom know?

BRAD: She trusts me. She knows I'll do it. I'll do it the day before we go back.

AMANDA: Well since you're here, you should join us!

Paul and I are reading *Othello* out loud, it's just better to do it that way. We could use a third actor. We'll read all the parts out loud.

BRAD: *Othello* is the one I wasn't going to read. I know the story. I saw the movie.

AMANDA: Still, it would just be fun, to read it with friends, right? You could be Othello!

BRAD: I'd make a better Iago.

AMANDA: That works too.

BRAD: I'm going solo on this one, Desdemona. Thanks anyway.

Amanda is visibly disappointed. Paul picks up on this.

BRAD: Hey, Amanda. I remember you weren't allowed to read *Black Boy* in honors last year. Your parents wouldn't let you, right?

AMANDA: Oh. Yeah.

BRAD: Not trying to make you feel uncomfortable. I'm just curious: Why is *Othello* okay? I mean, Othello's black.

AMANDA: You know, I don't know. It's Shakespeare. It's a play.

BRAD: Doesn't have 'black' in the title.

PAUL: Brad...

AMANDA: No—it's okay. It's fair. My parents may not know what it's about. If it's Shakespeare...you know with them that's like, automatic green light.

BRAD: There's so much sexual stuff in Shakespeare. All over.

AMANDA: Is that so? (*beat*) Maybe uh...maybe you could...

BRAD: Show you sometime?

AMANDA: That's not—

BRAD: I wouldn't mind.

Silence.

PAUL: Uh, so...Amanda. You want to head in?

AMANDA: Yes. Last chance, Brad.

BRAD: I'm around, Amanda. Whenever you need me.

AMANDA: Paul. When I was at your front door a guy showed up.

PAUL: A guy?

AMANDA: He didn't give his name but he was kind of short and growing a mustache. He had a big box with him.

PAUL: Alex.

BRAD: Sounds like Alex.

PAUL: It has to be.

BRAD: Short. Growing a mustache. That's him all right.

PAUL *(to Amanda)*: Do you know if he's still out there?

AMANDA: He headed up the street.

PAUL: Shit.

AMANDA: Who's Alex?

PAUL: A guy I thought I was done with.

BRAD: Did he graduate this year or last year?

PAUL: Last year. '95.

BRAD: When was the last time he showed up here?

PAUL: Four years ago. Last time he and I talked. We had it out then. I thought I made it clear he wasn't welcome.

AMANDA: Should I go? This guy sounds creepy.

PAUL: Did he seem creepy to you when you met him?

AMANDA: Sort of. More like intense. Really intense and focused. He really wanted to talk to you, Paul. It was like this urgent need for him.

PAUL: Sounds like Alex.

AMANDA: I'll go so you can deal with him. We can do this another time. That way Brad can be a part of it too.

PAUL *(beat)*: Oh no. No. I'm not going to switch my schedule around because this guy who lives up the street from me who I had a falling out with is demanding to see me now. I'm not dropping everything—my friends, my summer coursework—for him. So what I'm saying is stay, Amanda. Stay. I'll go check if he's out front. Be right back.

Paul gets up and heads off stage. Silence.

AMANDA: What's with the sword?

BRAD: I ran my stepdad out of the house today.

AMANDA: Oh. For good?

BRAD: Yeah, for good.

AMANDA: That's cool. I heard he was really mean. Wasn't he some kind of trucker or something?

BRAD: Construction worker, but that's pretty close.

AMANDA: So why'd you bring the sword over here? It's not even in a...what's it called...

BRAD: Scabbard.

AMANDA: Right. Aren't you scared someone's going to see you walking down the street with a sword?

BRAD: Amanda. Come on. Like anyone's out there to see me, and if they did would they even care?

Amanda looks all around. Her gaze goes over the short fence.

AMANDA: We really do live in the country.

BRAD: It's not called the City Gems. (*pause*) Hey, what do you think of Paul? I mean really think of him? (*beat*) I don't want to get personal...

AMANDA: Are you asking if I like him?

BRAD: You were the star of *Frankenhunk* and *Bride of Frankenhunk*.

AMANDA: So were you.

BRAD: I just figured with as much time as you two spend together…Maybe he'll join your religion.

Amanda laughs.

AMANDA: Paul? Yeah, right. He's going off to Hollywood to become some big shot director and forget me and the Saints.

BRAD: Time will tell.

AMANDA: It always does. (*beat*) But to answer your question: Paul and I are just good friends. I don't think we'll ever…you know.

BRAD: Got it. Just wondering.

AMANDA: I think you and I are good friends too.

BRAD: I suppose we are.

AMANDA: Are you and him having problems? He mentioned you were upset about him selling his Nintendo and all the games last year.

BRAD: I see it as something that held us together.

AMANDA: He's getting rid of his role-playing games too.

BRAD: What, really?

AMANDA: I'm not sure I was supposed to tell you that. Oh boy.

BRAD: Amanda…

AMANDA: He told me he's going to take them all to this place in the El Cajon mall. Game-something.

BRAD: Gametowne. That bastard. All the role-playing games? Every single book?

AMANDA: He didn't tell you?

BRAD: Why would he tell me? He knows how angry I'd be.

AMANDA: You're really angry.

BRAD: These things, they're *us*, Amanda. And he's just getting rid of us like that. I don't want to be an Indian Giver but...

AMANDA: What?

BRAD: I gave him some of those books. He knows that.

AMANDA: What do you have there?

BRAD: E.

AMANDA: Oh. Is that...medication?

BRAD: You are so damn straight-edge.

AMANDA: Hey. I can't help it.

BRAD: You were raised that way. I know. *(beat)* I can't imagine what it would be like to have religion be such a huge force in my life, I mean every waking and unwaking moment just be breathing it in and out. What's that like?

AMANDA: Like I'm underwater. And I can't breathe.

Brad offers two of the pills from the bag to Amanda.

BRAD: This'll help. Guaranteed to open up your airways.

AMANDA: No thanks.

BRAD: Would it help if it's night and you're with me?

AMANDA *(beat)*: Uh...

The sound of gravel crunching off-stage alerts them to Paul's approach. He enters.

PAUL: Did you really just push drugs on Amanda, Brad?

BRAD: You got me.

AMANDA: I didn't take any.

PAUL: She can't even have a soda, man. And you're pushing E on her?

BRAD: Don't get all high and mighty here, Paul.

PAUL: I saw you from the window—

AMANDA *(quickly)*: You took a while, Paul. Did you talk with him?

PAUL: I walked out to the front, and sure enough he was headed down again, like he's on a timer.

AMANDA: Did he have the box?

PAUL: He did. When I said you were in the backyard, Brad, he wouldn't open it. Wanted to open it in front of you too.

AMANDA: So is he coming back here? Should I go?

PAUL: I wouldn't let him in the house. Told him he had to go around to get back here. But he has to wait a few minutes. Go inside, Amanda. I'll make sure we don't drag it out with him.

AMANDA: If you're sure.

PAUL (*to Brad*): You should get out of here.

BRAD: Why? Sounds like he wants to see me just as much as he wants to see you.

PAUL: There's something about the box. When I mentioned you were over he got even more agitated than usual.

BRAD: I'm not leaving, Paul. Someone has to finally tell him off.

PAUL: I'll tell him off. I'll do it again, this time for good.

BRAD: Don't blame me if I don't exactly believe that's going to happen.

PAUL: It is. This is the end.

BRAD: Beautiful friend, the end.

AMANDA: I don't know about this, guys.

PAUL: Please, Amanda. Stay. It'll be quick, like pulling a band-aid off real fast, and he'll be gone and we can get to *Othello*.

AMANDA (*pause*): Fine. But if it doesn't look right to me...

BRAD: Call the cops? Then wait half an hour till the CHP shows up. (*pause*) It'll be fine, Amanda. Trust me.

Amanda exits. Paul hesitates before sitting down next to Brad.

PAUL: I can't imagine what he would have in a box.

BRAD: A severed head? He could *Seven* us.

PAUL: He's not *that* crazy, Brad.

BRAD: Oh he's crazy, Paul.

PAUL: I know. But still.

BRAD: Remember when he told us about the hit lists he'd made of all the students and teachers...

PAUL: Yeah...

BRAD: And that was in middle school.

PAUL: He was eighth grade and we were sixth.

BRAD: Remember...remember the gun he showed us?

PAUL: Of course. I told my parents about it.

BRAD: You would have.

PAUL: Hey. It was a good excuse not to hang out with him anymore.

Brad laughs.

PAUL: What?

BRAD: Nothing. It's just you needed your parents' permission not to hang out with that loser.

Silence. Paul yanks at the grass.

PAUL: He might be bringing the gun over now. (*pause*) I sure thought he had the gun last time I saw him.

BRAD: Four years ago?

PAUL: I was sure he had it, and I thought he might even use it. He was so forceful. I didn't say he could come over, he just did, as if he'd never picked up on any of the hints I'd been dropping him for years.

BRAD: What'd I say? Screw loose.

PAUL: He was wearing this heavy ski jacket, puffy.

BRAD: A parka.

PAUL: Yeah. A parka, even though it wasn't all that cold out. And as he was talking to me one hand stayed in his jacket pocket the entire time, and I swear, Brad, I swear something was poking through the fabric of the pocket, aimed at me.

BRAD: You think he really had the gun.

PAUL: I think he really had it.

BRAD: And he really was going to use it? Shoot you on your front doorstep, in broad daylight?

PAUL: Why not? It would've been easy. With his background, everything he did, that day we were over at his house and he showed us, so casually—yeah, I think he would've used his gun.

BRAD: And actually kill you.

PAUL: The guy can do it. It may be the only thing he's good at.

BRAD: How'd you get rid of him?

PAUL: I cried. In front of him. Claimed I had a death in the family. A distant relative that nevertheless was dear to me.

BRAD: And he believed you?

PAUL: He left. It must've worked.

BRAD: Good acting, Paul.

PAUL: Well. It's kinda like what Kafka wrote...

Brad sits up straight and looks out over the fence.

BRAD: He's coming.

PAUL: Time's up, I guess.

BRAD: That's a big box.

PAUL: He said he needed to give me some stuff. (*pause*) Last chance to get out.

BRAD: He's not going to open it without me here. You said so yourself.

Brad and Paul make as if they're relaxed. Off-stage sounds of something heavy dropping, the fence creaking, footsteps in the *gravel. ALEX enters carrying a large cardboard box. He wears a long-sleeved collared shirt, jeans and tennis shoes. He glances at the samurai sword standing straight up in the lawn, then looks from Paul to Brad. At last he sets the box on the lawn next to the sword. Histrionically he exhales and wipes the sweat from his forehead.*

ALEX: Whew. I'm carrying my whole life in there.

BRAD: Hey, Alex.

ALEX: Hey. Glad you're here. This was supposed to be between just me and Paul, but for you I'll make an exception.

BRAD: Gee. I'm touched. (*beat*) So what's in the box, Alex?

ALEX: A celebration.

BRAD: A celebration, huh. That's funny. Because I'm celebrating something too.

ALEX: What's that you're celebrating?

BRAD: I ran my stepdad out of the house today. For good.

ALEX: Huh. Congratulations.

Alex glances at the samurai sword.

BRAD: Now we're just chillin'...talking, listening to some Jethro Tull....

ALEX: Jethro Tull, huh.

BRAD: You know Jethro Tull?

ALEX: Yeah I know 'em. What album?

BRAD: *Thick as a Brick.*

ALEX: That's a good one.

BRAD: Maybe you know then.

Brad looks to Paul for approval. Paul makes a gesture of neutrality.

BRAD: So do you know what happened to this kid on the cover, in the newspaper here? This "Little Milton" kid?

Brad hands the liner notes to Alex. Alex looks at the album cover and smiles.

BRAD: Paul thinks he's dead, he died when he was like, eleven or twelve maybe, but I think he's probably alive in England somewhere, holed up in some apartment in London, writing his magnum opus or something. Shunning all human contact, like J.D. Salinger. What do you think?

ALEX: What do I think? I think you guys should surf the Web.

BRAD: The Web?

ALEX: The World Wide Web. This kid's not real.

PAUL: Not real?

BRAD: What?

ALEX: It's a total publicity stunt put on by the band. You'd know that if you guys were on the Net.

PAUL: The Net?

ALEX: The *Internet*, fools. I found it out months ago. I've been on the Internet a lot since my parents got it. Don't your parents have it, Paul?

PAUL: They're getting it in a couple weeks. (*pause*) He's really not real?

ALEX: The whole thing's not real. The band wrote the song—lyrics and all. What did you think—this ten-year-old kid could actually write a poem like that, and win a prize like this, and you didn't think this could have been a fake photo, and this newspaper could have been made up too? Bands do it all the time.

Alex tosses the liner notes at Brad.

BRAD: Well, shit.

PAUL (*to Brad*): I can't believe it. The Internet...

ALEX: It's all there. Everything is. You know that TWA flight that crashed last month?

PAUL: What about it?

ALEX: One of the passengers spontaneously combusted. That's what brought it down.

BRAD: Bullshit.

ALEX: It was headed to Rome.

PAUL: Brought down by the Pope, huh. Don't believe everything you read, Alex.

ALEX: It's not reading, Paul.

PAUL: What's in the box, Alex?

ALEX: I want it to be like the old days, guys. I really do. But she's here.

PAUL: She left.

ALEX: You're a terrible liar, Paul.

BRAD: Hey, Alex. My bet is it's a severed head.

PAUL: Brad—

ALEX: Why would you say that?

BRAD: Why not?

ALEX: I would never do such a thing. Severed head...

BRAD: It's not outside the realm of possibility.

ALEX: What are you saying, Brad? What are you saying?

PAUL: Alex...Brad. Tone it down. Both of you.

ALEX (*to Paul*): I thought I wanted him here but I see that's a mistake. (*to Brad*) You're a disgrace.

BRAD: That's funny coming from you.

ALEX *(to Paul)*: He knows this song you've been listening to's a joke. He's a joke. So, why?

PAUL: I guess...well, we're friends.

Alex ignores this last comment. He opens the box.

ALEX: So, Paul. I got a proposition for you.

PAUL: What's that, Alex.

ALEX: I'm gonna give you some things.

PAUL: Okay.

Alex takes out an armload of oversized softcover books and sets them in the grass beside the box.

ALEX: It's all there.

PAUL: What is?

ALEX: All my role-playing games, for one.

PAUL: Okay...

ALEX: All the Robotech, the Palladium, the Ravenloft, D&D...

PAUL: You're giving them to me.

ALEX: And—

BRAD: Hey, Alex. You know one of the signs of suicide—

Alex, who has his hand in the box, whips out a Walther PPK pistol and aims it at Brad.

PAUL: Jesus, Alex!

Brad puts a hand up and looks away.

ALEX: Don't think I won't do it, Brad. I'll do it! I shoulda done it that day.

BRAD: Go ahead.

PAUL: What day?

ALEX: He wouldn't have told you, the coward. (*to Brad*) Tell him.

BRAD: Put the gun down and I will.

Alex hesitates, but sets the gun on top of the books already out of the box.

PAUL (*to Brad*): What's going on, man?

BRAD: Nothing.

ALEX: 'Nothing' is your favorite word, isn't it?

BRAD: It's not a big deal! You bring up the stupidest shit, Alex. It was just one day.

ALEX: Killing your stepdad's not "some stupid shit."

Silence.

PAUL: Brad.

BRAD: All right! All right! (*pause*) So that day we saw the gun for the first time, that gun right there, and you and I left...remember how I stayed back a little?

PAUL: Yeah, a little. I guess...I thought you were right behind me.

BRAD: You didn't notice. You were so set on getting home and probably locking the door...

PAUL: Hey.

BRAD: But that's what you did. (*pause*) And I stayed. I stayed with this guy and told him more than I told you today, more than I've told anyone about The Badger. And he listened —something I knew you wouldn't do—

PAUL: Tha—

BRAD: Just listen! I needed this, don't you see? I needed to fight back then. And I saw that gun, and I thought—

ALEX: When you were twelve.

BRAD: Yeah, I thought, that's the only way. That's only ever been the only way. And so I—

ALEX: So me and him make a deal. We'll ambush his dad —I'll help him with the ambush—if he agrees to hang out with me more than he hangs out with you.

PAUL: What?

ALEX: He agreed. Must've really wanted to kill his father—

BRAD: —My stepfather—

ALEX: —because he hung out with me a lot of the rest of that winter and all through the spring.

PAUL: That's why—

ALEX: Why he never called you then? It must've been tough for you, feeling how it feels, for once. I swear you just about called me, I think.

Brad and Paul exchange a charged look.

ALEX: It took all that time to plan it, just about. By the summer it was like, we better do it or we're never gonna do it. Brad here kept wanting to change the plan, which I see now was just an excuse. (*pause*) So it's June now, right, and we have the day and time, too. This guy, this stepfather, toughest-looking guy I've ever seen, is out there walking with his shirt off, down Pressman.

PAUL: Jesus.

ALEX: And he's walking these two big dogs, these mastiffs, like wolves, and they're snapping and straining on the leashes, and I have this vision of Hades, the god with Cerebrus, all he needs is a third dog.

BRAD: We were in the ravine.

ALEX: That's right. You know how on one side of Pressman is the road and on the other side is that creek that runs all the way along, and it's so dense with trees and other things in there, so dark, how you and me used to play there—don't you? Well that's where we were, crouched, just peeking over the ridge to the road...

BRAD: And the Badger was coming by.

ALEX: We could see him through the trees, walking our way. A pretty clean shot. He had his shirt off, I could see where I would've got him. But Brad here was the one holding the gun. I was right next to him, whispering Do it, do it now! Come on!

BRAD: He was so close.

ALEX: You were so close, coward. You even had one eye closed taking aim. Sure had me fooled. I was breathing on you by that time.

BRAD: I had a song in my head.

ALEX: Fat lot of good it did you. Song...

BRAD: And I was thinking, Do it! Do it, Brad! End him. The punches, the kicks, the bending, the pushing—

ALEX: The words—

BRAD: All of it I could end.

ALEX: But did you? (*pause*) You let him go. You let him pass, riding that chariot on into another five years of your personal living hell. And you let him. Because you wanted it.

BRAD: Fuck off.

ALEX: Secretly, you did. You got off on it. I saw it in you then.

BRAD: You were fucking screaming at me. He could've heard.

ALEX: And seen his own son with a gun, intended for him. He would've made the—

Brad scrambles to his feet and rushes Alex. Alex reaches for the gun but before he can touch it Brad has shoved him over.

BRAD: For the last time: he is not my dad!

ALEX: Got it. Got it.

Brad turns from Alex, who is just sitting up, and takes up his sword. This he carries back to Paul. Brad stops beside Paul and remains standing, looking at the sword. Alex gets to his feet but remains beside the box.

ALEX: After that I knew you weren't my friend. A true friend wouldn't have failed like that. (*beat*) But we had a good run, didn't we, Brad? Showed Paul here the two of us could band against him and show we didn't need him.

PAUL (*to Brad*): Then you came back.

ALEX: And I thought, So it didn't work out with Brad. So what. I'll go back to Paul. It's not a defeat. It was just a...just a sojourn. That's all. Paul was my only real friend anyway from the beginning. Brad—just a distraction. I was here first.

PAUL: That's enough, Alex.

ALEX: When I go back to you, you've changed. You're different. You were getting different toward me already, even before the gun—but now. It's like I'm permanently wait-listed, in limbo with you. You didn't even put me in your movies, and all I asked for was a bit-part, a tiny role. What gives? What gave? I thought the gun would do it. I thought, with the gun, they'll have to be my friends. They'll like it, think it's cool, give me the same respect I give them, for once. I mean, what guy doesn't want to hold or at least see a gun? What guy?

Paul points to himself.

PAUL: This guy.

ALEX: That gun would've been cool in the movies you made.

BRAD: We already had a gun, Alex. One that wouldn't kill anyone accidentally. A BB pistol. I told you.

ALEX: So it was this gun. The danger of it. That's what did it. It backfired. That's what did it. Your fear of this thing.

Alex picks up the gun and looks at it.

ALEX: I thought to myself, in all the time after, Was it the gun? Was it this? (*to Paul*) Hell, you can have this. I'm giving it to you along with everything else in there.

PAUL: I don't want your gun, Alex.

ALEX: It's a gift.

PAUL: No.

ALEX: I was never going to shoot you, Paul. Even though I could've. I could've but I didn't. I was never going to shoot you, please know that. My dad wouldn't have cared. Six years ago, he'd lost track of this even then. It was in his room, but he wanted me to use it. He wanted me to have it. I'm trying to tell you this because I love you as a friend, my only friend in this whole damn town, you know? And it's not like my dad's going to know you have it. He hasn't asked about it in three years. The last time was—I had it by that time, it was mine, it's mine now and so I'm giving it to you as your best and truest and only friend. Your first friend.

Alex, incredibly emotional, holds the gun out to Paul. Paul does not get up. Finally, he shakes his head.

ALEX: At least take the RPGs...

PAUL: Why are you doing this?

ALEX: I'm leaving. I'm going away. You know I graduated. And then this summer I went ahead and signed up for the army. I'm going to do it. If there's another war with Iraq, to finally take out Saddam, I'll be there, on the front lines.

PAUL: Good for you.

ALEX: And my parents are moving. They're going to Virginia. All the way across the country...I've lived all my life here, I don't really want to leave it, I know I won't have anything like the experience I've already had here, with you guys. And so I want you to keep these things for me, Paul. Save them, please, for when I come back. The RPGs...eventually I'm going to have each and every one laminated, so it's in absolute perfect condition, and I'll have them lined up on the shelf, in order, and I can take them down whenever I want and show my son and say, This is what I played when I was your age. Now here.

PAUL: I'll take the RPGs, Alex, but you're taking the gun with you.

ALEX: That doesn't make sense. The army's gonna give me a better gun, a more powerful gun. They may even give me two. Why would I need this gun? You need this gun. For protection, from your enemies.

PAUL: What enemies, Alex.

ALEX: Remember when that big guy, on the bus, remember when we got off the bus at the stop here and he just kicked you, in the nuts—do you remember?

Paul nods.

ALEX: And you were crying so hard. I felt so bad for you, I had to help you, even though it was over between us by then. I helped you home...

Silence.

ALEX: If you had this gun....

PAUL: I wouldn't have shot him.

ALEX: But to just have it.

PAUL: You would've killed him.

ALEX: I wouldn't kill anybody.

PAUL: You're going to be killing people in the army, Alex. Saddam?

ALEX: Just take it.

PAUL: No.

ALEX: Take it and I'll leave.

PAUL: The RPGs only—and anything else you have in there. Just not the gun.

Resigned, Alex turns back to the box. Still holding the gun, he takes more softcover books out.

BRAD: I wouldn't give him the RPGs.

Alex pauses, waits. Paul looks at Brad, baffled.

BRAD: He's selling all of his. They're in a box in his room right now. (*pause*) Who's to say he won't sell yours too.

ALEX (*to Paul*): Is this true?

Paul shrugs, nods.

BRAD: You may be gone a while. When you get back...

ALEX (*to Paul*): All of them?

PAUL: All of them.

ALEX: Even *The Compendium of Weapons and Armor*?

PAUL: I'm...sorry. I didn't know—

ALEX: You didn't think to consult me about this?

PAUL: Alex—

BRAD: He sure as hell didn't think to consult me. I'll take all of 'em off your hands, Paul. Oh, but that would mean if you hang out with me you might see them, be embarrassed by their presence.

PAUL: Jesus. I didn't—

ALEX: Think? No. You're not thinking now. You're just doing the same thing you always do.

PAUL: Oh yeah? What's that?

ALEX: Please. You're such a pleaser. You can't just hate anyone, can you? Always gotta please everyone. Hell, you'd probably side with Saddam if you went to war.

Paul laughs and shakes his head, incredulous.

ALEX: You've never had the guts to say what you really

want to say to me. Tell me off—like you probably wanted to tell me off the day we met at the pool, our moms meeting...That's right: you're so terrified of making a bad impression. Such fear. So eager to please. Eager to please your parents, your teachers, the bus driver, the lifeguards, the guy at the corner store who makes the sandwiches, my parents—everyone, everyone, everyone you come into contact with you have to please or you'll feel guilty and think you're an awful person. Everyone has feelings—even I have feelings—and you'll do anything not to hurt them. Which is why instead of calling me up and saying, Hey, Alex, I know we haven't talked in a while, but I was just going through my RPGs that we've been playing since pretty much we met, and I wanted you to know I'm giving them up, and I'd like you to have first crack at them—instead of doing that you avoid, you avoid because that's another way you feel you can please people. Please them by avoiding the problem. What they don't know—

PAUL: I want you to know something, Alex, and that's you left out someone from that list you mentioned, and it's a good thing because I never tried to please him, and you know why? Because he was never my friend. He's missing from that list. He's you, Alex. You.

ALEX: We were never friends.

PAUL: We're not friends now. We're never going to be friends.

ALEX: No, we're not.

PAUL: I'd take a thousand Brads over you any day.

ALEX: We're not, we're not, we're not, we're not...

As Alex repeats these two words his face darkens. He speaks to the ground, then suddenly to the sky. He hurls his words in peals of half-laugher, half-crying.

ALEX: We're not! We're not! We're not!

Paul looks at Brad, who grips the sword tighter.

ALEX (*calm-sounding*): You know if you're a Muslim. You know if you're one of them...and you have a knife, or a sword, and the knife or the sword is sheathed, but someone angers you, someone says something so piss-poor awful it makes you just want to—if that happens, and you draw your sword, you unsheathe it, then you have to, you must use it. Once it's out, you must. It's Muslim law. A fact. If the Muslim doesn't draw blood, he's committed a sin. So, Brad, I don't suppose you want to sin.

BRAD: Do I look Muslim to you?

Alex levels the gun at Brad.

ALEX: You look dead to me.

PAUL: Fuck, Alex, don't—

Alex is crying now.

ALEX: I would never shoot you, Paul.

PAUL: Alex, put—

BRAD (*to Alex*): Do it, fucker! Go on! There's not enough action in all the world to satisfy you.

PAUL: Brad!

BRAD: You gonna shoot me? You gonna seriously *shoot* me?

PAUL: Brad, run!

BRAD: Aim high, army man. I can take it. But can you take this?

Brad steps forward and swings the samurai sword so that it comes within a foot of Alex's face. Alex keeps the gun aimed but steps back. There is real fear in Alex's tear-saturated eyes.

PAUL (*realizing*): Brad, don't! It's not loaded! It's not loaded, is it, Alex? Is it loaded?

A short sharp BANG sounds as Alex fires. The bullet strikes Brad in the chest. Brad screams and staggers backwards. The sword drops. Brad falls in the grass. Now only a frightening wheezing issues from his mouth. Then: the blood. Paul kneels beside him.

ALEX: You had to ask! You had to ask!

Alex throws the gun in the box and exits. Sound of gravel crunching, the fence creaking. Silence.

PAUL (*in tears*): Brad...Oh, God, Brad...

Brad's breathing is growing shorter and shorter. His eyes have glazed over. Blood seeps from under his shirt. Paul puts his hand to Brad's chest and feels. He looks around wildly, out in the distance.

PAUL: Someone! Help!

Amanda rushes out. In tears, she kneels beside Brad's body, clasps her hands, and prays.

Blackout.

Do You See What I See

TIME: July 1995

PLACE: Along a wooded highway in San Diego's North County

SETTING: The interior of a car. Four chairs serve as the seats: two in front, two in back.

CAST:

Jill, 16
Amanda, 15
Jacob, 18

Do You See What I See

JACOB is in the driver's seat (miming steering); JILL is in the passenger seat next to him. AMANDA is in the backseat. The stage is dark, signifying night, with the only light meager on the car's three occupants. Occasionally bright beams will cross the three faces, indicating a passing car.

Silence. Then:

JACOB: Was it worth it?

JILL: You didn't hate it that bad. (*beat*) Did you?

JACOB: It wasn't that bad. But that's not why I asked. I asked because I have to prepare Amanda.

AMANDA: Prepare me for what?

JACOB: For when you get home and your parents grill you as to why you're late and why you saw a movie you're not allowed to see.

JILL: Have a little faith, Jacob.

JACOB: Faith?

JILL: Or optimism. Or something. Something besides this.

JACOB: Realism, Jill. That's what this is.

JILL: Can we just talk about the movie?

JACOB: Sure. Two thumbs up?

AMANDA: I liked it. I think it was worth it.

JACOB: Worth the drive.

AMANDA: Yes.

JACOB: Worth the traffic.

AMANDA: I wasn't driving.

JACOB: Worth the repercussions.

JILL: Lay off her, Jacob. We're only a little late. Traffic was bad. It's a long drive back. They're going to understand.

JACOB: They didn't understand about the coffee.

JILL: What?

JACOB: Nothing. I let that slip.

Jacob eyes Amanda in the rearview. She looks uncomfortable.

JILL: Whatever.

AMANDA: It's not whatever. It hurt.

JILL: Amanda—what?

AMANDA: He saw. I didn't know you'd seen, Jacob. And you didn't say anything.

JACOB: I know not to get involved with your parents.

JILL: What happened? Coffee?

AMANDA: You didn't know because I wiped it off before I saw you. I cleaned myself up before first period. I had time. But it hurt. It wasn't like it was lukewarm.

JACOB: I saw the steam.

AMANDA: You couldn't have done anything.

JILL: What *happened*? Will one of you tell me already?

AMANDA: You tell her. I can't.

JACOB: Still too painful.

AMANDA: Still too embarrassing.

JACOB: I see Amanda getting dropped off at school in, what, February this year? Her mom was of course driving. It's at the front of the school, but it's also really early so there's like no one around. No adults. Just me and a couple of other guys.

AMANDA: It was Wednesday. We had class that morning.

JACOB: And I don't know how it happened, how she found it, like was your backpack open?

AMANDA: It was closed, but I left it behind and she reached for it and when she touched it...

JACOB: Oh, she felt the heat.

AMANDA: She must've.

JILL: Okay...

JACOB: So when Amanda gets out of the car her mom starts *screaming* at her. Totally unhinged. And she's going on about coffee coffee coffee, and I see through the front window of their car she's holding up this thermos, it's not that big, but she opens it and...

AMANDA: Tell her. You've gotten this far.

JACOB: She throws it in Amanda's face.

JILL: No.

JACOB: That's what happened.

JILL: That's unreal.

JACOB: It was *real*, Jill. I saw it. Amanda got it full in the face.

JILL: She threw the coffee right in your face.

Amanda nods.

JILL: I can't believe it. I didn't notice? I mean later that morning. Your face must have been raw. Scalded.

AMANDA: It took a lot of water. I was good about cleaning up.

JILL: Oh...Manda, I'm...

AMANDA: I learned never to sneak coffee to school.

JILL: I can't believe you would sneak coffee to school. How did you...

AMANDA: Someone in class gave it to me on our way out.

JILL: Someone at the ward? Who?

AMANDA: I'm not telling.

JILL: Not even me.

AMANDA: I'm sorry, Jill. Not even you.

JACOB: Here's the thing: her mom threw the coffee in her daughter's face, and then she drove off. Yeah. She just drove off. Peeled out of there. (*beat*) I'm guessing she didn't mention it when you got home that day.

AMANDA: She never mentioned it. She still hasn't. (*beat*) Then again, she knows I'll never try it again. So she doesn't have to mention it.

JILL: Unreal. I know your mom. That could have...

AMANDA: If it was any hotter, yes.

JACOB: So, Jill, knowing that now, do you still think they're going to understand?

JILL: Amanda's not sneaking coffee.

JACOB: But she snuck the movie she wasn't allowed to see.

JILL: To which we have our story straight, right? (*beat*) Right?

JACOB: Yes. Of course.

JILL: I swear, Jacob, if you let it slip we saw—

JACOB: We saw *Apollo 13*. It's what you wanted to see.

JILL: Exactly.

JACOB: You're a *big* Tom Hanks fan.

JILL (*beat*): I sure am.

JACOB: Even though you've only seen *Sleepless in Seattle*.

JILL: Hey. That was actually pretty risqué for a PG movie. Wouldn't you agree, Manda? They talked about orgasms.

AMANDA: Jill! Don't say that word!

JILL: What, orgasm?

AMANDA: Don't say it!

JILL: Orgasm orgasm orgasm orgasm orgasm orgasm.

JACOB: That's a lot of orgasms.

AMANDA: I can't believe you, Jill.

JILL: Oh come on, Manda. You didn't turn the movie off the moment you heard the 'o' word. You were enjoying it.

AMANDA: I was not. Not that part.

JILL: You blushed scarlet, but you didn't turn away. I admired you for that. *(to Jacob)* Manda's face was redder than if she'd had coffee thrown in it.

AMANDA: Not fair, Jill.

JILL: None of it's fair, is it? *Sleepless in Seattle*, we're allowed. Never mind the sex talk. *Apollo 13*, of course. But no *Forrest Gump*! It's PG-13!

JACOB: Hanks was better in *Philadelphia*. You missed out on that.

JILL: That one's R. And plus I was fourteen when you went to see it.

JACOB: I could've gotten you in. You just didn't want to see it.

Silence.

AMANDA: That's the one where he's...

JACOB: He's gay. And has AIDS.

JILL: You stayed through the whole thing.

JACOB: I did.

AMANDA: And you liked it?

JACOB: It was great. Very...emotional. Moving. Well-directed. Well-acted.

Silence.

AMANDA: Well I'll say the same for *Batman Forever*.

JACOB: Emotionally moving?

AMANDA: Yes! You're such a cynic...

JILL: That's what you are: a cynic!

AMANDA: One big cynic.

JILL: You hated it.

JACOB: I didn't hate it. I do think it lacked the things that made the first two better. The whole idea of Batman is that the world is dark and weird. Tim Burton understood that.

JILL: I'll take Val Kilmer over the other guy.

JACOB: "The other guy"?

AMANDA: Michael Keaton.

JILL: How do you know that?

AMANDA: I just do.

JILL: Val Kilmer's a better Batman. He's better-looking.

AMANDA: Definitely in agreement back here. (*beat*) But I thought Chris O'Donnell was the best-looking.

JILL: Mmm. Yes. I won't argue. (*beat*) What do you think, Jacob?

JACOB: What do I think?

JILL: Yeah. Val Kilmer or Chris O'Donnell?

AMANDA (*in a rush*): Why make anyone choose? They're both *equally hot*. Why not just a Val Kilmer-Chris O'Donnell sandwich?

JILL: Amanda! Get your gutter-mind back to where it belongs already! (*beat*) So, I need an answer. Which? Val

Kilmer or Chris O'Donnell? Or are you sticking with Michael Keaton?

JACOB: In terms of what?

JILL: In terms of, you know...

Silence. Jacob keeps his eyes on the road, unable to look at either girl. He grips the wheel.

AMANDA: What's going on here?

JACOB: Drop it, Jill.

AMANDA: Jill?

JILL: I will. I'm sorry. I can be not myself sometimes.

JACOB: You're only ever yourself.

AMANDA: I don't understand.

JACOB: You don't have to, Amanda. My sister's dropping it.

AMANDA: Jacob. Are—

The sound of a helicopter above. During the following exchange the whir of the blades intensifies in volume and reverberations.

AMANDA: No.

JACOB: I thought so.

JILL: That's ridiculous. They wouldn't—

JACOB: Realism, Jill. You think that's the Batcopter? Val Kilmer's gonna descend on his utility belt?

A spotlight shines into the car's interior. Amanda ducks the light to lie across the two chairs in back.

JILL: It's my Goddamn birthday!

AMANDA: *Jill!*

JILL: I swear—where do your parents get the idea—why are you down? You need to let them see you!

AMANDA: It's better they *don't* see me!

JILL: Why? So they think you're dead? Then we're really in for it.

AMANDA: It's just me, Jill. I'm the one who has to answer to them.

JACOB: It's me they're worried about. The fact you're with me.

AMANDA: You're an approved chaperone, Jacob. Why would that have changed?

Jill glances at Jacob, who concentrates on the road ahead. The whirring reaches a crescendo. The reverberations shake the car, while the spotlight floods the compartment. Amanda screams.

AMANDA: They see everything!

The light withdraws swiftly, as if Amanda's words were a kind of exorcism. Gradually, the whirring of the helicopter fades. At last, no sound remains save that of passing cars.

JILL: You can sit up now, Manda.

AMANDA: I don't think so.

JILL: It's gone.

AMANDA: I'd rather lie back here. It feels better this way. I feel better.

JILL: Okay. (*beat*) They were probably looking for someone else.

JACOB: Oh you think?

JILL: They know your car. Why didn't they pull us over just then?

JACOB: A helicopter's going to pull a car over? When has that ever happened in the whole history of the human world?

JILL: It has. I know it has. (*beat*) Manda, are you okay back there?

AMANDA (*her voice faint*) I'm fine.

JILL: Are you feeling okay?

AMANDA (*still faint, now edgy*) I'm fine. Leave me alone.

Jill twists around to look in back.

JILL: Are you—

Jill spins back around. Her eyes are wide.

JACOB: Is she okay?

JILL: She's fine. Leave her alone.

JACOB: Good thing we're almost to Anomar. That's why they didn't keep on us. We're almost home.

JILL: That must be it.

JACOB: Are *you* okay?

JILL: Oh. Yeah. The movie never ends, just like the song says.

JACOB: Don't stop believin'.

JILL: That would be it.

JACOB: You haven't actually died on us back there, have you, Amanda?

AMANDA (*her voice a sigh*): *No...*

JACOB: How's the movie going? The one that guy Paul's making? What's it called?

JILL: *Frankenhunk.*

JACOB: *Frankenhunk*. How come you're not in it?

JILL: I don't know. I don't know Paul all that well. He and Amanda, they live in the Country Gems and...

JACOB: And we townies just don't fit in with them, do we? Hey, Amanda—

Amanda sits up. Her face is flushed. Jacob observes her in the rearview.

JACOB: You look sick, like you've come down with something. Do you have a fever?

Amanda places a hand to her forehead.

JACOB: Are you hot?

AMANDA: I feel pretty hot.

JILL: I think you're going to be fine, Amanda.

AMANDA: I think I am too.

JACOB: We're almost home. There's the sign now. (*to Jill*) Something funny?

JILL: Something definitely is, Jacob.

JACOB: Well. What? Are you going to let me in on it?

JILL: I don't think so. Unless you want to, Manda.

AMANDA: No...This is between me and Jill.

JACOB: And doesn't involve me.

AMANDA: Nope.

JACOB: And won't get me in trouble.

AMANDA: No trouble from us. Promise.

JACOB (*beat*): It's times like this when I think you two are the actual siblings instead of Jill and me.

JILL: You'll be fine, Jacob.

Silence. After a few moments, Jacob turns the wheel and stops the car.

JACOB: There you go.

Amanda opens the "door" and gets out.

AMANDA: I don't see Mom and Dad. Yet.

JILL: Maybe you lucked out.

JACOB: Heavenly Father gave you a pass. A gift.

AMANDA: Yeah sure.

JACOB: Call it Christmas in July.

AMANDA: I'll let you know if I'm alive in the morning. See you, Jacob. Thank you, Jill. Bye.

JILL: Bye, Manda. Good luck.

Amanda smiles, waves and exits. Jill and Jacob remain in the idling car. Silence.

JACOB: Was she...

JILL: Human? Yes, Jacob. She was human. Is human. Will stay human, I hope.

JACOB: I hope the same for you, Jill.

JILL: And you, Jacob. Please don't forget.

JACOB: Never. (*beat*) Happy Sweet Sixteen, sis.

Slow fade to darkness.

END

About the Author

David Ewald is the author of the novels *The Thief of That*, *The Book of Stan* and *He Who Shall Remain Shameless*, the collection *The Fallible: Stories*, and the cycle *Great Awakenings & Other Plays*. He is a graduate of the College of Creative Studies at the University of California Santa Barbara and the MFA creative writing program at the University of Notre Dame. He writes, teaches and parents in California's Central Valley.

davidewald.net

Old Little Theater, Goleta, California.
December 4, 1997. Performing John Updike's
"A & P."

www.ingramcontent.com/pod-product-compliance
Lightning Source LLC
La Vergne TN
LVHW041059150826
845673LV00007B/1843

* 9 7 9 8 9 8 8 9 7 9 5 6 2 *